WINOOSKI SUBDIVISION

NORTHWARD TRAINS			STATIONS	SOUTHWARD TRAINS		
Miles from Burlington	Yard Limits			Office Signals	Siding Car Capacity	Length of Siding in Feet
0.2	0.9	⎫	BURLINGTON......Z		YARD	YARD
2.8		MBS	2.6 WINOOSKI......		23	1394
8.0	6.5	⎭	5.2 ESSEX JCT.......PYZ (Jct. with Roxbury Sub.)	SX	YARD	YARD

Rules 321-323 applicable.
Rule 105A not applicable.

WINOOSKI SUBDIVISION FOOTNOTES

1 RULE MODIFICATIONS

1.1 System Special Instruction 2.0 applies over the entire subdivision.

1.2 Burlington Yard: Rule 104 is modified as follows: Yard switches equipped with locks, except main track switches, are not required to be lined for normal position after having been used.

2 GENERAL FOOTNOTES

2.1 BURLINGTON – Stop must be made by all movements using Astroline Oil Company track at least 50 feet from entrance gates.
All C.V. movements on Vermont Railway main track must be made as prescribed by Rule 93.
Vermont Railway yard limit board is located approximately one mile south of College Street.

2.2 TRACK NO. 260 MILEAGE 1.73
Train and engine crews operating over unloading bridge at the McNeil Woodchip plant, use CAUTION on account of the close side clearance on the trestle. Scaffolding will not clear caboose monitors or awnings on locomotives.

ROXBURY AND SWANTON SUBDIVISIONS

NORTHWARD TRAINS				STATIONS	SOUTHWARD TRAINS			
REG. 623	MILES FROM WINDSOR	YARD LIMITS			SIDING CAPACITY	LENGTH IN FEET	REG. 624
PSGR							PSGR
DAILY							DAILY
05:00	14.8			WHITE RIVER JCT...PW 17.4	YARD	YARD	22:30
	32.2			...SO ROYALTON....P 7.2	82	4894	
	39.4		⎫	......BETHEL ....P 6.4	66	3944	
	45.8			......RANDOLPH ......P 14.9	72	4344	
	60.7		MBS	......ROXBURY......P 15.8	87	5263	21:15
	76.5			...MONTPELIER JCT ..PY 9.6	78	4672	
	86.1			......WATERBURY 7.3	84	5038	21:00
	93.4			......BOLTON......P 5.9	77	4630	
	99.3		⎭	......RICHMOND...... 9.2	84	5012	
	108.3			...ESSEX JCT ......PY (Jct. with Winooski Sub.)	66	3966	20:30
	119.1			......MILTON...... 10.8	71	4269	
	127.4	131.2		......OAKLAND...... 8.3	84	5040	
07:35	132.1 Miles from St. Albans 0.0	↔		...ST ALBANS...CKWVZ 4.7	YARD	YARD	20:00
07:45	1.5	2.6		...ST ALBANS...CKWVZ 1.1	YARD	YARD	19:10
	5.6		⎫	......NORTH JCT ...Z 4.1			
	9.5		MBS	......FONDA...... 3.9			
	15.6			......SWANTON...... 6.6	75	4477	
			⎭	...EAST ALBURGH 2.4			
08:30	18.0	23.8		......ROGERS...... 7.4	74	4417	18:15
	25.4			......CANTIC......RYZ			

Rules 321-323 applicable.

THE
Central Vermont
RAILWAY

THE Central Vermont RAILWAY

A Yankee Tradition

By Robert C. Jones

Volume VII   1981 – 1995

THE NEW ENGLAND PRESS
Shelburne, Vermont

On the cover: This beautiful photograph taken by Jim Shaughnessy on February 3, 1995, the last day of CV operations, vividly illustrates the changing order. Trailing the three CN road units on northbound Train 323, manned by engineer Mike Flanagan and conductor David Boardman, are five New England Central GP-40's that will go into service for the new owner the following day. Using a cornfield located about a mile north of Richmond, Vermont, as a vantage point and 4,083-foot snow-covered Camels Hump as a background, Jim Shaughnessy made this historic late afternoon photograph as the sun was rapidly setting on the Central Vermont.

© Copyright 1995 by Robert C. Jones

All rights reserved. No part of this book may be reproduced or transmitted in any form or by any means, electronic or mechanical, including photocopying, recording, or by any information storage and retrieval system, without permission in writing from the publisher, except by a reviewer, who may quote brief passages in a review.

Printed in the United States of America

First Edition
Library of Congress Catalog Card Number: 89-196493

For additional copies of this book or for a catalog of our other New England Press titles, please write:

The New England Press, Inc.
P.O. Box 575
Shelburne, VT 05482

This Volume is dedicated to:
The many thousands of employees and officials who have devoted a major portion of their lives to the Central Vermont Railway—in its offices, stations, boardrooms, and shops, along its track, and on its trains, in fair weather and foul, through good times and bad. Each has played an important role in making the Central Vermont Railway a "Yankee Tradition" for the past 150 years.

Preface and Acknowledgments

This volume concludes the long history of the Central Vermont Railway, which previously has been documented by this author in six volumes covering the 1830-1981 period. *Volume VII* backtracks slightly to 1980 to cover the Central Vermont's final fifteen years of operations in text and illustrations.

The first six volumes were published by Sundance Publications Limited of Silverton (now Denver), Colorado. In recent years, however, Sundance has on hand numerous Colorado railroad publishing projects that may require several years to complete. Thus, Dell McCoy, the president and owner of Sundance Publications, graciously gave up the rights to this series of books so that this volume could be made available in a timely fashion by another publisher. For this gesture, as well as for other helpful considerations, I wish to thank Dell McCoy of Sundance Publications Limited.

New England Press of Shelburne, Vermont, the publisher of my popular three-volume Railroads of Vermont series, has enthusiastically accepted the task of publishing *The Central Vermont Railway, Volume VII*. In doing so, they have made every attempt to produce a volume that will be compatible with the other books in this series.

Central Vermont, Volume VII chronicles a very difficult and often sad period in the history of this venerable New England transportation institution. Owned by the Grand Trunk Corporation, itself a creation of the giant Canadian National Railway, the CV has quite naturally found itself subjected to the policies and mandates of the parent company. Deregulation, declining business, and labor-management tensions and disagreements were only a few of the factors that contributed to the continuous downsizing and lowered morale of the CV's workforce during these last fifteen years. In addition, during this time the Grand Trunk Corporation on more than one occasion announced its intent to sell the CV—the GTC, too, was in a downsizing mode.

Difficult times notwithstanding, the CV continued to maintain its track in excellent condition. Normal running speeds for freight trains continued to be forty miles per hour and passenger trains operated at fifty-nine miles per hour. Few would argue that the CV's track was among New England's best.

During the last year or more of the CV's life, its pending sale largely preoccupied the time and thoughts of all those directly involved with the operation of the railroad, as well as that of politicians and the general public. After countless hearings, lengthy deliberations, political intervention on all levels, union charges and countercharges, and court and regulatory body decisions, the Central Vermont was sold to RailTex of San Antonio,

vii

Texas. The CV's last day of operations was February 3, 1995, and RailTex Corporation's New England Central Railroad began running trains the following day.

The full history of the CV's final fifteen years is documented in words and photographs on the following pages. Many people have contributed information and material to make this book a fitting conclusion to the CV's long history.

Information was gleaned from contemporary newspaper accounts, company publications, professional journals, railfan publications, and annual reports.

The first draft of the text was read and critiqued by former general manager Chris J. Burger and trainmaster Paul K. Larner. Both clarified various points and provided additional information. Chris Burger, in addition, provided a number of slides for use in this project.

The majority of the Southern Division photographs came from the cameras of Bob Barnett, Rich Barnett, Steve Carlson, Ken Houghton, and Dan Foley. Their contributions did much to ensure appropriate pictorial coverage of the CV's operations south of Brattleboro and provided a good overall pictorial balance to the book.

Internationally known award-winning railroad photographer Jim Shaughnessy was a major contributor to this volume. Jim has contributed a great deal to many of my other publications, and once again his enthusiastic and gracious response to my request for photo material is highly valued.

Alan Irwin, M.D., perhaps the CV's all-around most knowledgable railfan, provided not only many great photos, but also spent hundreds of hours researching and producing the locomotive rosters that appear in this volume. Alan acknowledges that Ken Lanovich of Chicago was a helpful source of roster information. Brian and Bonnie Irwin often accompanied their dad on his photo trips, and their work also appears in this volume.

Long-time CV employee and resident historian Jim Murphy once again provided photographs and information, in addition to doing darkroom work on some of the material used herein.

Fred Bailey, unquestionably one of the best and most active rail photographers in this region, is a major contributor to this book. In addition, the very detailed information he provided with each slide or photograph was an invaluable help in writing informative and accurate captions. It is unfortunate that space constraints allowed for only a fraction of Fred's contributions to be included. Through Fred's guidance and support, Fred's wife Gracie has become interested in rail photography, and some of her fine shots are included.

Leo Landry's marvelous color slides have a prominent place in this volume. Particularly noteworthy are his carefully set up night shots. Ken Houghton contributed several fine photos and also made available some of Bill Gleason's work.

Other major contributors to this volume include Nathaniel Cobb, Tom Hildreth, Gary Knapp, and Roger Wiberg. This work would have been lacking had their many fine contributions not been available.

Others who graciously provided material include Ed Betz, George Dutka and the Central Vermont Railway Historical Society, Joe Dufresne, Jr., Dick Gassett, Kevin Smith, Scott Whitney, and Steve Zuppa.

Andrea Gray handled the design and layout work in a most professional manner. A special thanks is due Mark Wanner of New England Press. Mark has been the director of this project from start to finish, and the very enthusiastic, knowledgable, and personable manner in which he has shepherded the project through its many complex phases is very much appreciated.

The finished book is, I trust, a fitting tribute to every person who contributed to it and to every former Central Vermont employee.

Robert C. Jones
Burlington, Vermont
August 1995

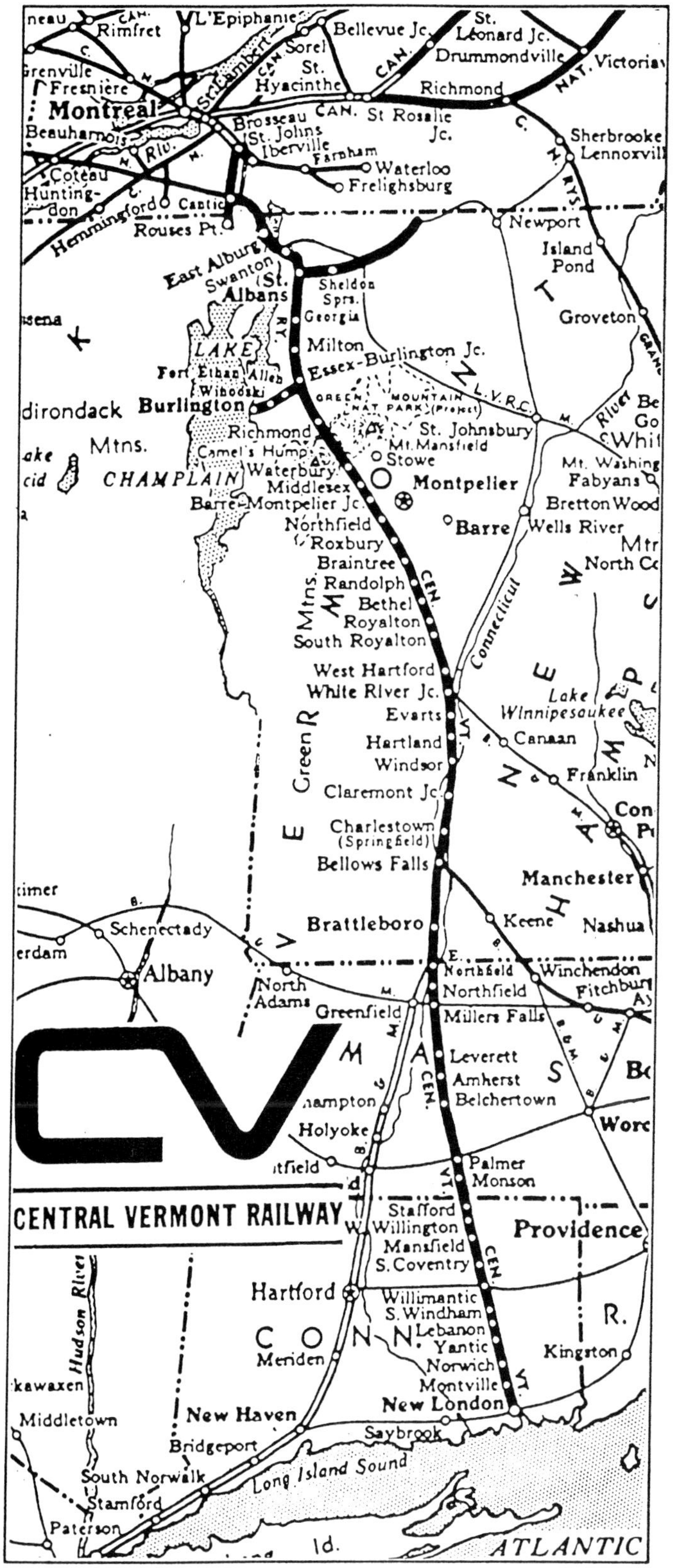
CENTRAL VERMONT RAILWAY
CV
Montreal
Rimfret
L'Epiphanie
Bellevue Jc.
St. Léonard Jc.
Drummondville
Victoria
Sorel
St. Hyacinthe
Richmond
Fresnière
Beauharnois
Brosseau
St Rosalie Jc.
St. Johns
Iberville
Farnham
Waterloo
Frelighsburg
Sherbrooke
Lennoxville
Coteau
Huntingdon
Hemmingford
Cantic
Rouses Pt.
Newport
Island Pond
East Alburg
Swanton
St. Albans
Sheldon Sprs.
Georgia
Groveton
Milton
Essex-Burlington Jc.
Fort Ethan Allen
Winooski
Burlington
Adirondack Mtns.
LAKE CHAMPLAIN
Richmond
Camel's Hump
Waterbury
Middlesex
Barre-Montpelier Jc.
Mt. Mansfield
Stowe
St. Johnsbury
L.V.R.C.
Montpelier
Barre
Fabyans
Bretton Wood
Wells River
Northfield
Roxbury
Braintree
Randolph
Bethel
Royalton
South Royalton
Green Mtns.
West Hartford
White River Jc.
Evarts
Hartland
Windsor
Claremont Jc.
Charlestown (Springfield)
Bellows Falls
Connecticut
Lake Winnipesaukee
Canaan
Franklin
Manchester
Keene
Nashua
Brattleboro
Schenectady
Albany
North Adams
Greenfield
E. Northfield
Northfield
Millers Falls
Winchendon
Fitchburg
Leverett
Amherst
Belchertown
Holyoke
Palmer
Monson
Stafford
Willington
Mansfield
S. Coventry
Providence
Hartford
Willimantic
S. Windham
Lebanon
Yantic
Norwich
Montville
New London
Kingston
Meriden
Hudson River
Middletown
New Haven
Bridgeport
Saybrook
Long Island Sound
South Norwalk
Stamford
Paterson
ATLANTIC

The 1980s through the first half of the 1990s was a dynamic, yet a very traumatic time for the Central Vermont Railway, a wholly owned subsidiary of the Grand Trunk Corporation (GTC). GTC was established in late 1971 as the holding company for the Canadian National Railway's American railroad subsidiaries—the Grand Trunk Western Railroad Company (GTW), the Duluth, Winnipeg & Pacific Railway Company (DW&P), and the Central Vermont Railway (CV).

So that the reader may have in one volume the history of the Central Vermont from the beginning of the 1980s to its demise on February 3, 1995, the 1980-1981 period that was briefly covered in Volume VI of this series will be reviewed here.

The Staggers Act of October 1980 deregulated the railroad industry and redefined competition. This benchmark legislation was intended, at least in part, to aid railroads in moving closer to parity with other industries on their investment returns. The deregulation of the industry's rate structure caused serious concerns about the long-term effects of this legislation, however. Simultaneously, the railroad industry faced extremely high rates of inflation and a recession in major segments of the economy, which resulted in a predictable decline in traffic.

In 1980, the Central Vermont operated about 365 miles of track in the states of Vermont, New Hampshire, Massachusetts, Connecticut, New York, and in the Province of Quebec. From an operational standpoint, the line north of White River Junction has long comprised the road's Northern Division, while the Southern Division includes all trackage south of White River Junction.

The CV recorded operating revenues of $20.8 million, an all-time high, in 1980, and a net income after taxes of $1.4 million. The company moved 57,000 carloads over its system during the year and employed an average of 412 people.

At this time, the CV had thirty locomotives on its roster, including six Grand Trunk-New England Lines units. The company's freight car roster totaled 1,284 cars. The motive power consisted primarily of Alco RS-11's and EMD GP-9's, although three SW-1200's and a lone S-4 were still in regular service. All of these elderly locomotives (No. 1511, the newest, was built in 1960) were leased from the parent Grand Trunk Corporation.

During the year, twenty of the road's locomotives were repainted. GP-9's 4924 and 4442 were rebuilt at the St. Albans shops, and 4924 also received dual controls at this time.

In September 1978, the CV initiated the *Rocket*, a dedicated intermodal (piggyback) train operating between St. Albans, Vermont, and Palmer, Massachusetts. Although this service was growing

1

Five Canadian National road locomotives provide the power for northbound Train 447 on a mid-summer day in 1980. The train, which is still in yard limits, is approaching the Jewett Avenue crossing, about two miles north of North Junction (Italy Yard). The lead unit, No. 2570, is flying white flags that designate the train as an "extra." (Roger Wiberg photo)

rather slowly, CV officials used this train to road test newer and heavier motive power that it was considering as replacements for the aging and worn-out RS-11's and GP-9's. One of the Vermont Railway's highly regarded GP-38-2's, No. 202 "George Aiken," handled the *Rocket* for ten days in early January 1980. The CV operating crews gave high marks to this visitor. The CV sent GT 4558, a twenty-three-year-old GP-9, to the VTR for use during this period.

In early December 1980, the CV began piggybacking highway milk tankers from northern Vermont to the Boston area. An arrangement with the Richmond Cooperative Creamery represented the first tangible evidence of the railroad's efforts to reclaim milk business lost to truckers decades earlier. Milk tankers loaded onto the train at St. Albans by 10:30 p.m. arrived at a Massachusetts plant for processing and bottling by 9 a.m. the next morning. Unfortunately, this traffic was shortlived. Within little more than a year, the customer changed its marketing procedures, and the business disappeared from the rails.

During the year, an ambitious $1.2 million track-improvement program saw CV crews install twenty-three miles of continuous welded rail at various locations, including the East Alburg trestle. Southern Division track forces replaced thirty-two thousand ties and spread sixty thousand tons of stone ballast. Italy Yard in St. Albans also received a long-overdue upgrading when seven thousand new ties were installed and the yard was reballasted. In all, more than 125 miles of track were surfaced and lined during the year.

In 1981, the *Rocket* came into its own. During the year, the company experienced a significant growth in intermodal traffic, due primarily to two factors: aggressive marketing and newly constructed intermodal facilities two blocks south of the CV's headquarters in St. Albans. This new $100,000, sixty-thousand-square-foot terminal doubled the company's trailer-storage and flatcar capacities. One hundred trailers and twenty-one flatcars could now be accommodated, and the eighty-nine-foot railcars could be loaded and unloaded on three tracks simultaneously.

Because of a power shortage, the CV leased the Vermont Railway's GP-38-2 No. 201 for a period of six days in January. No CV unit was sent to the VTR during this time.

During the year, lumber distribution facilities were established at Sharon, Vermont, as well as at

South Windham, Connecticut, and Palmer, Massachusetts. Some 27,500 carloads of Canadian and western lumber were unloaded at these and other points in 1981. In addition, the marketing personnel began encouraging Canadian customers to truck lumber to CV intermodal points to take advantage of the growing piggyback service.

In mid-March 1981, the CV began using pushers for the first time since the days of steam. Six locomotives were normally assigned to heavy southbound Train 444 in order to get it up Roxbury Hill, while four units could handle the same train from Roxbury to White River Junction. Two units were removed from the head end and placed at the rear, where they could be cut off at Roxbury to run light the seventy-four miles back to St. Albans. The four head-end units then continued on to White River Junction, where heavy tonnage for the Boston & Maine was set out, and then to Brattleboro with the rest of the train.

Trainmaster and road foreman Roger Livingston was sent to the Delaware & Hudson to learn first-hand how that road operated its pushers on heavy trains over Richmond Hill. CV officials estimated this plan would result in savings of nearly $300,000 in the company's annual locomotive fuel bill.

The CV's operating rules allowed a maximum of twenty-four powered axles (six four-axle locomotives) on the head end of a train, and the twelve-thousand-ton trains that soon appeared on the scene required additional power. Thus, these exceptionally long and heavy trains were powered by six units on the head end and two pushers on the rear.

In June, Phelps-Dodge Corporation's new copper wire manufacturing plant—the country's largest—became fully operational at Norwich, Connecticut. Some of the raw material used by this facility came from Chicago and was delivered by the CV via St. Albans. Some also arrived at New London by barge, and from there it went to Norwich by rail over thirteen miles of the CV's Southern Division.

Five new lumber customers located on the Southern Division in 1981, as well as Vermont Castings on the Northern Division at Randolph, Vermont. In addition, the large cement plant at

Southbound Train 444 is winding through Essex Junction, Vermont, in the spring of 1980. A Boston & Maine unit is the leader on this day. (Roger Wiberg photo)

The CV's Rocket, *a dedicated piggyback train, is crossing the Sugar River Bridge north of Claremont, New Hampshire, in June 1980. This spectacular structure has provided the setting for countless photographs over the years. (Scott J. Whitney photo)*

Train 447 is just coming off the north end of the long East Alburg trestle at a maximum allowable speed of ten miles per hour during the summer of 1980. The U.S.-Canadian border is about four miles ahead of the train. The track in the foreground is the former CV branch to Alburg and Rouses Point (New York). (Roger Wiberg photo)

4 THE CENTRAL VERMONT RAILWAY

Belchertown, Massachusetts, expanded its facility during the year.

CV track crews utilized newly purchased machinery in laying nearly twenty-one miles of welded rail in 1981. This brought the total of welded rail on the system to sixty-two miles. Seventy-eight-foot sections of rail were welded into 1,014-foot lengths by Lewis Rail Service of St. Albans. The first continuous welded rail in Vermont had been installed by the CV at Braintree in 1978. That year, 4.5 miles were laid, followed by 13.2 miles in 1979 and 23.3 miles in 1980. In addition to the new rail, thirty-five thousand ties were installed and thirty-seven thousand tons of crushed rock ballast was spread in 1981.

The company installed a fire detection device on the venerable three-quarter-mile-long wooden pile trestle across Missisquoi Bay between West Swanton and East Alburg. This unique fire alarm system makes use of linear thermal detection wire in an environment that ranges from -40 degrees to 120 degrees Fahrenheit. This critical structure, the victim of several previous fires, links the Canadian National's Quebec lines with those of the CV and the east coast of the United States.

This structure was so heavily damaged by fire in 1950 that rail traffic had to be rerouted for several months while repairs were being made. Unfortunately, the CV-owned detour route (the St. Armand Subdivision) was torn up and no longer remained an option in an emergency situation. The new warning system was installed at a cost of approximately $50,000, a figure that also included training for two CV employees who would inspect and service the system.

In August, the intermodal *Rocket* began handling U.S. mail between Montreal and Springfield, Massachusetts. It was the first time mail had traveled over the CV since Vermont's last railway post office was terminated with the discontinuance of passenger service on September 3, 1966. About twenty highway trailers of mail were soon being handled weekly, with shipments moving in both directions.

Despite a national economic recession, 1981 proved to be the best year in the company's long history from a financial standpoint. From revenues of $24.5 million, the CV derived a $3.1 million after-tax net income—also a record. The revenue

The I-95 overpass dominates this August 31, 1980, scene at New London, Connecticut, where the CV interchanges cars with the Providence & Worcester Railroad. The CV's modest yard here borders the wide Thames River and Long Island Sound. The turntable served a four-stall enginehouse at this time. (Jim Shaughnessy photo)

B&M trains pooling power with the Canadian Pacific Railway and operating on CV rails via trackage rights brought some interesting locomotives to the CV at times. This October 1980 meet at Brattleboro features trains powered by Canadian Pacific Alcos as leading units. The Chesapeake & Ohio GP-35 was on lease to the CP. (Fred G. Bailey photo)

from forest products, $11.1 million, constituted nearly one-half of the total, and it represented a record for this commodity.

On December 17, in a most disconcerting incident, engineer Hubert Smith, a thirty-two-year CV veteran, nearly lost his life while operating a freight train near Northfield, Vermont. He was struck in the chest by a bullet fired from a sniper's rifle. Emergency surgery removed the bullet, which had lodged near Smith's heart. The ensuing police investigation produced evidence indicating that the act had been premeditated.

Then, on the following March 10, another CV engineer, Bob Luman, was shot above the jaw at the same location. Later the same day, still another locomotive was fired upon at the same spot. This time the gunman missed, and engineer George E. Gay escaped unharmed.

Vermont State Police apprehended a twenty-one-year-old Norwich University senior fifteen minutes after this latest incident. Fortunately, both Smith and Luman fully recovered from their injuries and returned to work. As for the sniper, two counts of attempted murder and five counts of aggravated assault were plea-bargained to a single count of aggravated assault. The gunman pleaded insanity and received a one- to two- year jail sentence—none of which was served!

6   THE CENTRAL VERMONT RAILWAY

The CV's northbound Rocket, *is approaching Springfield Station (Charlestown, New Hampshire) on a cloudy November 7, 1980. Tom Hildreth took the photo of this unusually short piggyback train with a 135mm lens at 2:30 in the afternoon.*

Train 447 is bound for Montreal behind four CV units during the summer of 1981. Italy Yard is only a couple of miles behind as the head end of the train crosses Conger Road at about 40 miles per hour. (Jim Murphy photo)

THE CENTRAL VERMONT RAILWAY 7

Southbound through freight Train 444 is passing wayfreight 554 in Essex Junction on April 16, 1981. Train 554 worked between St. Albans and White River Junction, normally with a side trip into Burlington also. Normally Train 444 had two pushers on the rear, although on this day GP-9 No. 4924 was working alone. The number of pushers was determined by the amount of interchange traffic for the B&M at White River Junction. Head-end power was determined by the tonnage going over Belchertown Hill in Massachusetts. (Alan Irwin photo)

Train operations on the CV in 1982 can be summarized as follows. Trains 26 and 27, Amtrak's northbound and southbound *Montrealer,* operated daily. Freight train No. 444 departed Montreal for Springfield, Massachusetts, seven days a week. At St. Albans, local cars were cut out of this train and others were added. CV crews handled Train 444 to White River Junction, while B&M crews operated it south of that point. This train returned northbound as 447. Generally speaking, most of the southbound cars were loads, while empties returned northbound.

Train 22, the *Rocket*, departed St. Albans for Palmer every afternoon, Sunday through Thursday. A Northern Division crew handled the train to White River Junction, and a Southern Division crew took it south from there to Palmer. There, the loaded trailers left the rails to continue on to Hartford and Boston markets. The empty trailers returned northbound Monday through Friday.

Train 553 operated as a local freight Monday through Thursday from St. Albans to Swanton, back to St. Albans, and then over the twenty-eight-mile Richford Branch to an important interchange with the Canadian Pacific Railway. On Fridays, this job worked only the Richford Branch, while on Saturdays it operated from St. Albans to Swanton and Rouses Point, New York, and return.

Train 554 ran to White River Junction on Mondays only and returned to St. Albans the same day as Train 555. On Tuesdays, Wednesdays, and Thursdays, 554 operated as a St. Albans-Burlington turn. This job also handled local switching chores as far south as Montpelier Junction. The Burlington turn did local switching in the Queen City, as well as making an important interchange with the Vermont Railway.

St. Albans' Italy Yard was handled by day, night, and swing crews. At White River Junction, one crew worked the yard Monday through Friday and also performed the local work between Hartland and Randolph.

8 THE CENTRAL VERMONT RAILWAY

For a time, the CV's short-lived intermodal yard south of the general office building in St. Albans was a busy facility. Jim Murphy's dramatic 1981 night photo shows a trailer carrying U.S. mail being loaded onto a CV flatcar.

A trailer carrying U.S. mail has been loaded onto the CV flatcar and a carman is securing the highway trailer on the car before the next one is backed into place. (Jim Murphy photo)

On the Southern Division, Train 560 ran as a local freight between Brattleboro and New London, Monday through Saturday. Train 561 operated northbound between these two points every day except Sunday. At Brattleboro, a yard switcher was on duty Monday through Friday from 10:00 p.m. until 6:00 a.m. Additional extra trains, of course, were operated as needed.

In 1982, CV track crews installed thirty thousand new ties on the mainline. In addition, 4.2 miles of welded rail was laid on the Richford Branch between Sheldon Junction and Enosburg. Why this lightly traveled branch—a rumored candidate for abandonment—was selected for this major track improvement project remains a mystery.

During the year, the Interstate Commerce Commission approved Guilford Transportation Industries' (GTI) acquisition of the Delaware & Hudson Railroad. GTI, the holding company of both the Boston & Maine and Maine Central, was now able to add a third regional carrier to its portfolio. Historically, the CV's major traffic flow has been from Eastern Canada to the New England and Middle Atlantic states, in part via connections with the Boston & Maine at White River Junction. Grand Trunk officials, quite understandably, became concerned that Guilford would prefer a longer haul on significant amounts of Canadian-U.S. traffic via the Delaware & Hudson rather than utilizing the CV-B&M route.

While the Grand Trunk Corporation did not formally protest this consolidation, it did ask the Interstate Commerce Commission to guarantee that the CV would be permitted trackage rights between East Northfield and Springfield, Massachusetts, that this trackage be maintained to a specific standard, and that Guilford be required to continue to provide the same frequency of service as that in effect at the time the merger was approved.

In December 1982, the board of directors of the Canadian National Railway decided to put its CV subsidiary up for sale. This decision was based on two things—the uncertainty of the CV's future

The town of Stafford, Connecticut, sponsored a train/boat excursion on July 26, 1981. Passengers boarded the train at Stafford Springs for a 50-mile ride to New London. There they boarded a ferry steamer for the 30-mile trip to Block Island, Rhode Island. (Robert Barnett photo)

A southbound Central Vermont freight train has just exited the tunnel under Burlington's North Avenue and is entering the CV's small waterfront yard during the summer of 1981. Vermont Railway cars are being stored on VTR trackage that was formerly the Rutland Railroad's scenic mainline through the Lake Champlain Islands to Alburg. (Roger Wiberg photo)

profitability and the acquisition of the D&H by Guilford. Although discussions with several potential buyers took place in the following months, no sales agreement could be reached.

Subsequently, in mid-May 1983, the directors of the parent company reversed their decision to sell the CV. In a prepared statement, they said that the four proposals that had been received from prospective buyers "did not justify divestiture on the part of the Canadian National" (Grand Trunk Corporation).

When the road was put on the market, Central Vermont GP-9's Nos. 4450, 4549, and 4923 were sent to the Grand Trunk Western for storage. They were returned to the CV when the "For Sale" sign was taken down.

Generally speaking, 1982 was not a good year for the CV. As the nation's economic recession continued, CV traffic dropped from sixty-one thousand carloads in 1981 to fifty-three thousand in 1982. Revenues declined an alarming $1.1 million. In addition, operating expenses for the same period increased from $18.3 million to $23.8 million. Seventy-five employees were laid off during the year because of what one official termed "pure economics."

Fortunately, there were a few bright spots for the railroad in 1982. Forest products, the CV's leading revenue producer, increased 50 percent over its record-setting pace of the previous year. Seven on-line distribution centers now received Canadian lumber for distribution by truck within a wide radius of each center.

The Independent Cement Company at Belchertown, Massachusetts, erected new silos during the year, a factor that was largely responsible for a 34 percent increase in this traffic. Piggyback traffic, which was extended to New Haven, Connecticut, in late October, showed a 25 percent increase over the previous year.

This service was inaugurated by a special train that carried forty shippers as well as railroad and government officials over the new route to New Haven. In addition to this new intermodal terminal, overnight intermodal service via the CV's dedicated piggyback train, the *Rocket,* continued between St. Albans and Boston. A close connection

Normally the CV's St. Albans-bound intermodal Rocket *got top priority from the dispatchers. On this Saturday morning in the early 1980s, however, the piggybacker was being held at East Northfield, Massachusetts, for an Amtrak special that is swinging off the Boston & Maine. The* Rocket *then followed the Amtrak special to White River Junction. (Fred G. Bailey photo)*

To test the feasibility of replacing its aging fleet of GP-9's and RS-11's with more modern power, the CV borrowed Vermont Railway's GP-38-2 No. 202 for testing purposes in January 1981. The 202 is working a short four-car piggyback train carrying several VTR trailers northward past the Bellows Falls station. (Fred G. Bailey photo)

12   THE CENTRAL VERMONT RAILWAY

Photographer Roger Wiberg was standing near the site of the long-gone East Georgia passenger station to take this photograph of Amtrak's northbound Montrealer *coming off the Georgia High Bridge in the fall of 1981.*

at Brattleboro resulted in the loaded trailers being delivered in East Cambridge, Massachusetts, via the B&M the next morning.

In 1983, the CV's Southern Division again experienced significant traffic growth. Lumber volume increased another 30 percent, primarily because a large lumber distribution terminal and a wood treatment plant located on line at Belchertown. On the Northern Division, a new woodchip loading site went into operation at Swanton, and Wyeth Laboratories built a new plant with a rail siding at Georgia, Vermont. The Swanton facility was the point of origin of the significant woodchip traffic to the Burlington Electric Department. Rail traffic at the Wyeth plant proved to be moderate, however.

For years, the Grand Trunk Corporation had frequently transferred locomotives of its various subsidiaries from one road to another as motive power requirements varied. In 1983, the last of fifteen Alco RS-11 units, Nos. 3606, 3607, 3608, 3610, and 3613, were sent from the Duluth, Winnipeg & Pacific to the CV in an effort to standardize power on the four GTC carriers. No. 3608 had been chop-nosed by the DW&P in 1979, while Nos. 3607 and 3610 arrived unserviceable—essentially junk. These two units were stripped of parts and cut up at St. Albans within a few months of their arrival.

On April 12, several carloads of newsprint on Train 444 derailed at East Alburg soon after the eighty-five-car southbound train crossed the border from Canada. The 7:15 a.m. accident, which occurred near the three-quarter-mile-long East Alburg trestle, caused the track to move four feet laterally for a distance of about 150 feet. As a result of the derailment, the northbound *Montrealer* was held at St. Albans, and its passengers were bused to Montreal.

The CV installed the Canadian National-designed yard inventory system to provide better control of freight cars. This system, which is capable of locating any rail car on the railroad in seconds, became operational on October 16. Field terminals were set up at five locations—St. Albans, White River Junction, Brattleboro, Palmer, and New London. CV officials estimated that this new computerized system would save the road approximately $200,000 per year in labor costs.

Another 2.3 miles of continuous welded rail was installed in 1983, and when this work was completed CV officials justifiably boasted that their mainline was "the best track in Northern New England."

A newly negotiated labor agreement provided for three- rather than four-man freight train crews under certain conditions. In addition, the agreement allowed the railroad to operate one-fourth of its trains without cabooses. Although the question of whether trains should be allowed to operate without cabooses became a persistent labor-management issue, the CV unquestionably did realize savings in switching time and equipment maintenance when cabooses were not used.

Operating revenues continued their decline during 1983—from $23.4 million to $21.2 million, as the company suffered a loss of $700,000—its first in nearly ten years. The 10 percent decrease in revenue was matched by a similar decrease in carloads handled. These decreases, CV officials felt, were the result of increased competition that had been fostered by deregulation. The reduced crew agreement, the computerized car control system, and the downturn in business combined to reduce employment from 373 in 1982 to 320 in 1983.

In January 1984, the Delaware & Hudson officially became a merger partner in Guilford Transportation Industries' 3,900-mile rail system. Both the CV and the D&H connected with the Canadian National to serve as carriers of international traffic moving to and from Montreal and Western Canada. Increased competitive pressure from this development as well as from trucks and other rail systems such as Conrail resulted in a 13 percent decrease in carloads handled during the year by the CV. Moreover, this competition seriously limited the CV's ability to raise rates to recover mod-

Indicative of the CV's top-notch track maintenance program is the beautifully ballasted and immaculately maintained yard trackage in St. Albans' Italy Yard in 1981. By the early 1990s, the three tracks on the left had been declared redundant and were subsequently removed. Switchers were busy around the clock at this time, with yard lists coming from clerks housed in the yard office at the right. (Jim Murphy photo)

The mandatory brake test completed, southbound Train 444 is coming down the freight main from Italy Yard and is about to pass the Amtrak station and the CV's general office building on its way out of town during the summer of 1981. (Roger Wiberg photo)

estly higher operating costs. The net result was that revenues declined for the third consecutive year and by year's end the CV had suffered a loss of $2 million, its worst year in decades.

In early April, general manager Phillip Larson notified the Interstate Commerce Commission that the CV was considering abandoning the twenty-seven-mile Richford Branch. Traffic from the large H. K. Webster feed mill at Richford had dropped drastically, and Larson noted that it was no longer economical for the railroad to continue providing five-day-a-week service on this line.

The H. K. Webster plant is located on the Canadian Pacific, about one mile from the CV-CP interchange point. Within a year, the CP's charge for handling a one-hundred-ton car of feed had jumped from $190 to $440. As a result, Webster's had turned to trucks, and there were now very few cars to handle. Larson noted that, although business had improved slightly with Boise Cascade's Missisquoi Pulp Mill at Sheldon Springs, there were virtually no other active rail customers on the branch.

In May 1984, the Central Vermont's dedicated piggyback service, the *Rocket,* was terminated—a victim of increased competition and deregulation. Even though the cabooseless intermodal trains operated with reduced crews, their cost advantages to the shipper were insufficient to counter truck competition, particularly from what became known in the transportation industry as "gypsy" truckers. These truckers usually operate independently of established trucking firms, and their low overhead enables them to undercut railroads and other trucking firms for a short, but critical, period of time. The CV simply could not meet this competition with rates that would make its intermodal operation profitable.

Since the inception of the *Rocket* in 1978, a net profit had been realized in only two months. The service was set up to handle forty to fifty trailers a day, but an average of only twenty had been transported. Seventeen workers were laid off when this piggyback service was terminated.

On June 29, 1984, a 12:40 p.m. derailment on the long three-span steel bridge over the Mis-

Locomotive repairs of all kinds were routinely handled by the CV's mechanical department personnel at St. Albans. On this day in 1982, Mike Bourdeau, Roger Garceau, and Louis Preston are changing a traction motor in the enginehouse backshop. (Jim Murphy photo)

sisquoi River at Sheldon Junction permanently terminated all CV operations on the Richford Branch east of this point. The rear four cars of a combined Canadian Pacific-Boston & Maine (GTI) detour train derailed at the east end of the bridge. This train, which had originated at Newport, Vermont, on the CP, was operating over CV trackage because a bridge washout on the B&M at Wells River, Vermont, had curtailed all operations on the B&M's Conn River Line.

The derailed cars caused major damage to the bridge's easternmost span, as girders from this span were pulled down by the accident and one penetrated the roof of a boxcar just ahead of the CP caboose. In the salvage operation, this section of the bridge was dismantled.

Detour agreement provisions indicated that GTI was responsible for the damages, but when payment was not forthcoming, the CV brought a $1 million suit against Guilford Transportation Industries in U.S. District Court in Rutland. The court reaffirmed GTI's liability, and subsequently a court of appeals decision also upheld the verdict and ordered GTI to pay the CV $600,000 in damages.

The CV was one of the first railroads to contact Amtrak to learn more about its Emergency Response Training Program. In May 1984, the railroad hosted James Reynolds, Amtrak's Operations Training Manager, who conducted a safety program for more than forty operating employees during his three-day visit. Among topics discussed were ways to cope with crises ranging from fires and derailments to electrical dangers. In addition to the CV employees, representatives from fire departments in several towns served by the CV attended evening sessions that focused on rail-

Power for Train 444 was moving toward Italy Yard on November 5, 1981. This photo was made during the CV-B&M power pool era, hence the B&M GP-9 in this consist. The two Vermont Railway GP-38-2's were borrowed by the CV for about ten days to see if two of these locomotives could replace three GP-9's. It was found that they could not. In exchange for the GP-38's, the CV loaned Nos. 4551 and 4558 to the VTR. (Alan Irwin photo)

A southbound CV freight is seen from the Route 63 overpass at Millers Falls, Massachusetts, at 1:00 p.m. on the afternoon of February 4, 1982. The two tracks on the right are the Boston & Maine's east-west mainline. (Tom Hildreth photo)

Northbound Train 561 is crossing the Quaboag River on its approach to the south end of Palmer Yard on April 14, 1982. Three GP-9's, Nos. 4925, 4558, and 4447, are handling the train. (Robert Barnett photo)

Engineer Bob Luman is at the throttle of GP-9 No. 4549 as Train 444 approaches Milton, Vermont, during the summer of 1982. (Roger Wiberg photo)

road emergencies that might occur within their communities.

Little did Amtrak and CV personnel realize the almost uncanny timeliness of these safety programs. Tragically, within a few weeks, the knowledge and skills acquired during these sessions would be utilized to the fullest.

On July 7, Amtrak's *Montrealer* derailed between Essex Junction and Williston, Vermont, killing five people and injuring 138. Early that Saturday morning, the crew of the northbound passenger train boarded at White River Junction as usual. Conductor Vernon Church was in charge of the train, while George Gay was the engineer. The rest of the crew was comprised of assistant conductor Paul Goulette, fireman Jeff Howard, trainman Randy Heald, and baggageman H. G. LeMay.

At 6:50 a.m., as the crew was preparing for the scheduled stop at Essex Junction, the train approached a section of track left suspended in midair by a flash flood. A culvert, which had successfully withstood the ravages of the infamous 1927 flood, had been washed away by a torrent of water that had rushed down the adjacent hillside.

The two locomotives and a baggage car passed over the washout, but the lead unit rolled over on its side. The second unit and the baggage car derailed. The next five cars—three sleepers, a coach, and a food service car—piled on top of one another in the washout. The leading truck of the next car derailed, but the rest of the train remained on the rails.

An estimated three hundred rescue workers from area fire departments and rescue squads responded immediately. The first to arrive carried their equipment a half-mile across a trestle over the Winooski River. Soon others were pushing their way through the dense woods to the tracks. Vermont Air and Army National Guard helicopters were on the scene only a few minutes after the derailment. The Army Guard, in fact, was in the process of leaving the nearby airport for two weeks'

The CV's piggyback train, with two GP-9's on the head end, is about to leave the St. Albans intermodal yard in June 1982. This train was given top priority by the CV dispatchers on its trips to and from Palmer, Massachusetts. (Roger Wiberg photo)

The CV crew has just interchanged cars with the Canadian Pacific at the south edge of Richford, Vermont, on July 21, 1982, and the six-day-a-week Richford wayfreight is on its way back to St. Albans with a relatively short train. This truss bridge spans the Missisquoi River about three miles east of Richford. This trackage was removed in late 1993. For many years, SW-1200 Nos. 1509 and 1510 were regularly assigned to this job. (Leo Landry photo)

A CV local is turning a car on the wye at Brattleboro on a dark, cloudy day in 1982. (Tom Hildreth photo)

training at Camp Drum, New York, and some pilots were airborne as the train crashed.

Rescue workers removed the passengers from the cars, some on stretchers, after passing them through car windows. About eighty people were taken by helicopter and bus to the Medical Center Hospital in Burlington, where one of the victims died in surgery. Others were taken to the Fanny Allen Hospital in nearby Colchester and to the Williston Armory, which served as an assembly point. Vermont Governor Richard Snelling, who was on the scene shortly after 8:00 a.m., stayed until midnight, using the authority of his office to speed the rescue operation.

Access to the site was a major problem. Local construction companies were quickly on the scene, however, clearing trees and bringing in hundreds of truckloads of gravel to build a road for rescue vehicles and for the huge crane that arrived later in the afternoon to move the cars from their tangle in the washout.

All day the awful question of how many people might still be trapped in the most-damaged bottom car had gone unanswered as Amtrak officials cross-checked passenger lists against the names of those being treated at the hospitals or seen at the armory. By early evening it was confirmed that two people were not yet accounted for. When rescuers, using large banks of floodlights to illuminate the scene, found them early the next morning, both were dead.

The final count showed that fatal injuries had been received by conductor Vernon Church of St. Albans, an Amtrak sleeping car attendant, and three passengers in what was the worst passenger train accident on the CV since 1887. Conductor Church, with thirty-eight years of service, ranked second in seniority among the CV conductors and was nearing retirement. He came from a family of railroaders, as have many CV employees over the years. Ironically, Vernon Church's father, Clyde, also a CV conductor, died in 1940 after being crushed while switching freight cars at Barre, Vermont. Vern Church was sixteen years old when his forty-nine-year-old father was killed.

Hulcher Professional Services, Inc., specialists in railway accident salvage work, arrived from Gettysburg, Pennsylvania, on Sunday at dawn after a seventeen-hour trip. Immediately augmenting the CV crew that was already working on the task of getting the railway open again, Hulcher began moving the derailed cars out of the way

The ruling southbound grade to Roxbury always required extra power, and in the early 1980s the CV placed pushers on the rear of the train. These locomotives were then cut off at the top of the grade and returned light (no cars) 72 miles to St. Albans. Here we see the rear of Train 444 on August 6, 1982, as it passes the St. Albans engine house with consecutively numbered 4923 and 4924 working as pushers. (Tom Hildreth photo)

THE CENTRAL VERMONT RAILWAY 21

Train 444 is passing the Amtrak station at Montpelier Junction on a hazy, warm day in August 1982. The order board above the operator's bay window indicates no orders are to be picked up today. (Roger Wiberg photo)

using specially equipped and counter-weighted D-9 Cats.

Meanwhile, about fifty CV track workers removed debris from the track, repaired the roadbed, and installed prefabricated panels of track. A new steel culvert was laid to replace the stone box culvert that had been washed out, and a large amount of fill was dumped to rebuild the roadbed. This work was completed at 10:15 Sunday evening, only about forty hours after the accident. A five-mile-per-hour speed restriction was placed on the site, and at 6:17 a.m. Monday morning the northbound *Montrealer* slowly passed. Later, at 3:45 p.m., southbound freight Train 444 also made its way through the area.

The National Transportation Safety Board (NTSB) was on the scene by mid-afternoon on the day of the accident to begin its investigation into the probable cause of the tragedy. They noted that unusually heavy rain—six inches in a five-hour span—had caused flash flooding and that a series of ten or twelve beaver dams had been washed away. This contributed to the flooding and the tremendous pressure on the culvert and roadbed. The derailment took place on a twenty-two-foot high fill, and evidence showed that water had backed up behind the fill and culvert to a depth of eighteen feet before the fill and culvert let go.

Material reviewed by the NTSB included a report indicating that the section of track on which the accident occurred had been inspected the day before and that no irregularity in the rail or roadbed had been reported. Also, Central Vermont inspectors had performed their regular physical examination of the stone culvert in June, and no evidence of structural weakness had been found at that time.

However, the investigators blamed Amtrak for operating locomotives without appropriate radio frequencies that could have made it possible to

22 THE CENTRAL VERMONT RAILWAY

notify the train crew of the severe weather conditions in the area. Following the accident, Amtrak installed weather radio monitors in its major operations centers and established guidelines for passing on weather information to train crews.

In another incident, four cars of a thirty-nine-car New London-Palmer Southern Division freight train derailed in Norwich, Connecticut, on July 26, 1984. All four cars were empty, but one—a propane tank car—had derailed when loaded the previous week only one hundred feet from the site of this most recent derailment. Officials speculated that track curvature and an undetected defect in this car were the culprits. Damage was estimated at $50,000, and Hulcher Professional Services was again summoned to perform the rerailing work.

Then, on September 8, more than two hundred tons of woodchips were spilled when four cars of a twenty-one-car southbound train bound for the McNeil Generating Plant in Burlington derailed only minutes after leaving the loading facility at Swanton on tracks leased from the Lamoille Valley Railroad. The derailment occurred about one third of a mile west of U.S. Route 7, and a farm road leading almost to the site was of great benefit in the clean-up work. Three of the four $52,000 cars overturned in the 4:30 a.m. accident, and Hulcher was once again brought to the scene. Most of the chips were picked up by a front-end loader and trucked back to Swanton. Hulcher made quick work of rerailing the cars, which were taken to the CV repair shop in St. Albans, and the line was opened on the third day.

There were, however, a few bright spots in 1984. Quaboag Lumber, which received more traffic that any other customer, moved to its huge new site in Barretts, Massachusetts. In addition, the Independent Cement Company at Belchertown expanded its facility, with a resulting increase in rail traffic.

Perhaps most important, though, was the woodchip traffic that commenced in April. Burlington's new McNeil Generating Plant, which produces electric power for the city, went on line as the largest wood-burning electric generating facility

Three GP-9's lead Train 562 past the unused South Coventry, Connecticut, depot on August 7, 1982. This train will end its journey in New London, 35 miles to the south. (Robert Barnett photo)

Southbound Train 444 is approaching Northfield, Vermont, in August 1982. Undoubtedly, pushers on the rear are assisting the head end power at this point. (Roger Wiberg photo)

The pushers on the rear of Train 444 are hard at work as the train is working its way up the grade just north of Roxbury. Roger Wiberg followed this train and took a number of photos of it between St. Albans and White River Junction.

24   THE CENTRAL VERMONT RAILWAY

To promote an extension of the Rocket *piggyback service to New Haven, Connecticut, via a connecting Boston & Maine train out of Brattleboro, CV and B&M GP-9's teamed up on a special train operated for shippers and other potential customers on October 27, 1982. Here we see this train passing the primarily inactive connection between the B&M's Conn River line and the Springfield Terminal Railway at Charlestown, New Hampshire. The large lumber shed of the Saxonville Lumber Company here has just burned to the ground, but it was later rebuilt. (Fred G. Bailey photo)*

in the country. It was designed to use five hundred thousand tons of woodchips per year as its primary source of fuel. The CV began hauling this material from a woodchip loading facility at Swanton to the generating plant in North Burlington, a distance of thirty-eight miles, in twenty-one-car dedicated trains. Each train carried nearly eighteen hundred tons of woodchips in specially built eighty-five-ton capacity cars, three to five days a week. Within a few years, however, the unit train was reduced to twenty cars, which have been handled in the consist of the Burlington wayfreight, averaging two round trips per week.

In recognition of the marketing effort displayed by the CV in working with Burlington Electric to develop this woodchip traffic, the railroad received *Modern Railroads* magazine's Golden Freight Car Award for Class II railroads. Over the succeeding years, this traffic has been a steady source of revenue for the company.

A significant change in labor negotiations occurred in 1984. CV management notified union officials that the company's uncertain financial outlook would make it impossible to continue to operate under nationally negotiated labor agreements where wage increases had been typically seven or eight percent a year for the previous five years. CV officials indicated that they would, therefore, negotiate independently with the twelve unions representing the CV's 290 employees. Three other New England railroads and eight national carriers had also decided to bargain locally.

Proposals were exchanged in July, and talks continued into 1985. The decision to "go local" in the negotiations process at this time proved to be a landmark decision. Agreements in which long-term job security provisions for CV employees were granted in exchange for minimal or no wage increases in subsequent years had long-term detrimental effects on management-labor relations.

Pushers were rare on CV rails south of White River Junction, but for a brief time in 1982–83 the Boston & Maine regularly assigned them to heavy Conn River trains operating between White River Junction and East Deerfield, Massachusetts. A GP-18 and GP-9 are pictured passing the Brattleboro station behind the caboose of a southbound B&M train. (Fred G. Bailey photo)

Restrictive work rules also negatively impacted on the efficiency with which this relatively small, struggling railroad could operate.

Operation Lifesaver, now a well-publicized safety program designed to reduce grade crossing accidents, was strongly supported in its early years by the CV, the Vermont Railway, and by Vermont's other rail lines. The CV's efforts helped to gain financial backing for the program from the State of Vermont. In 1984, the CV ran its first Operation Lifesaver special train over the line, thus attracting public attention to the various problems caused at grade crossings and by trespassers on railroad property. Later, the CV and other Vermont railroads utilized three cars on loan from Amtrak to carry 150 law enforcement officials, legislators, and railroad personnel from Montpelier to St. Albans. The message to these officials was clear: tougher enforcement of existing crossing and trespassing laws will save lives!

Although competition from trucks and other rail systems continued to erode the CV's newsprint traffic, the rate of loss slowed somewhat in 1985. On the positive side, two newsprint distribution centers opened in Massachusetts during the year—Maple Leaf at Barretts and New England Warehouse at Monson.

The joint B&M-CV freight service known as the *Washingtonian* was canceled in 1985, and the familiar sight of B&M and CV power operating together between St. Albans and Springfield, Massachusetts, became a thing of the past. These trains had been classified at St. Albans with a caboose near the middle of the consist and another at the rear. The mid-train caboose separated the B&M cars that were set off en route from those that would continue their journey to CV destinations.

With the termination of the B&M-CV interchange at White River Junction, the CV began hauling a larger percentage of traffic to Palmer and other points on the Southern Division. The bridge traffic formerly interchanged with the B&M at White River Junction was now interchanged with Conrail at Palmer. This virtually doubled the CV's length of haul, which resulted in a significant increase in revenue per carload.

A shift to on-line origination or termination of traffic continued during 1985. Four years earlier, for example, two-thirds of the CV's business was bridge traffic—that is, cars that were taken from one carrier, hauled over all or part of the CV system, then given to another railroad. By 1985 this figure had dropped to 37 percent. Given the weakening of CV's traditional traffic flows because of competition and imports (automobiles, for example), it was essential to pursue aggressive marketing activities to generate this on-line traffic. Three categories of commodities that showed gains in 1985 included lumber, chemicals and fuels, and copper—up 14, 11, and 64 percent respectively.

A very important development in CV traffic patterns in 1985 was the return of intermodal (piggyback) traffic. A contract was negotiated with Quaboag Transfer, Inc., to move trailers-on-flatcars between St. Albans and Palmer, Massachusetts. Quaboag provided the locomotives (Alco RS-11's 3606 and 3611, which were purchased from the CV), and the cars, while leasing ramping facilities at both terminals. The CV, for its part, provided the track and operating crews. Before going to Quaboag, the two locomotives were reconditioned and painted in Quaboag's colors—medium metallic green with a gold logo and lettering.

Loaded trailers were hauled southbound three days a week, and the empties were returned to St. Albans on alternate days. The contract specified that trains of fifteen or fewer cars were to be operated without a caboose and by a two-man crew. Longer trains were to be handled by a three-man crew and a caboose. This "rent-a-train" concept earned the CV a marketing award from *Modern Railroads* magazine for 1986, the second consecutive year the CV was so recognized.

In early July 1985, Train 447 struck a tractor trailer on the North Duxbury Road crossing a few

Using Interstate 89 as a vantage point, Tom Hildreth photographed this southbound train near Hubbard Corners in Georgia, Vermont, on February 11, 1983. There is a good bit of snow on the ground, although there has not been a fresh snowfall for several days.

The CV's piggybacker Rocket *makes its way southbound between the former B&M station and the photogenic feed mill at Westminster, Vermont, on a beautiful afternoon in the early 1980s. With a cloud of black smoke, Alco RS-11 No. 3609 is whisking the train through town at 40 miles per hour. (Fred G. Bailey photo)*

On a very snowy day in the early 1980s, the CV's Rocket *holds the siding at Claremont Junction, New Hampshire, while a southbound B&M freight train passes on the mainline. (Fred G. Bailey photo)*

Train 444 is passing the Palmer station on March 15, 1983, behind five GP-9's. The rails stockpiled here had been replaced by the CV's ongoing continuous welded rail project. (Tom Hildreth photo)

Four CV units are bringing Train 444 into Palmer on April 4, 1983. The lead locomotives are crossing the busy Conrail mainline, and the 4925 is about to pass the former B&M passenger depot. (Tom Hildreth photo)

THE CENTRAL VERMONT RAILWAY 29

miles north of Middlesex, Vermont. The flat-bed truck, which was loaded with spools of wire, stalled on the crossing. When the driver was unable to get the truck off the tracks, he jumped from the cab shortly before it was demolished by the train. Damage to the lead locomotive was minor, and the train was able to continue its run.

Later in the month, a southbound Burlington wayfreight derailed at Essex Junction as it was leaving the mainline and heading onto the branch. Three empty cement cars and two loads of grain near the middle of the seventeen-car train derailed as the train was crossing Park Street. The 5:30 p.m. accident tied up crossings at one of the state's busiest intersections for about two hours. One of the loaded cars turned onto its side, while the other four derailed cars remained upright. A locomotive arrived from St. Albans at about 7:00 p.m. to haul the caboose and the nine rear cars back to that point, while the undamaged head three cars on the train later continued on to Burlington. A local contractor's heavy crane was used to move one of the cars away from the mainline, as crews worked over the weekend to clear the damaged equipment and repair the track.

Vandalism resulted in a serious derailment of Train 561 near Leverett, Massachusetts, on the evening of August 8. Although the three crew members escaped injury, four locomotives and seven of the train's forty-seven cars were derailed at a siding switch. Someone had tampered with the switch, causing the derailment and resulting in damages of about $250,000 to the locomotives, cars, and track. The CV immediately offered a $10,000 reward for information leading to the arrest and conviction of the person or persons responsible, but, unfortunately, no one has ever been apprehended.

On September 27, southern Connecticut was lashed by Hurricane Gloria. Fearing a repeat of the disastrous 1938 hurricane, CV officials and employees worked frantically to take all possible precautions to minimize damage to railroad property. Computers and other expensive equipment

EMD SW-1200 switcher No. 1509 idles at the Palmer yard office on a sunny day in April 1983. This unit was built in April 1957 as the CV was belatedly making its final steam runs. The CV sold No. 1509 to the Ellis & Eastern Railroad in May 1989. (Leo Landry photo)

30   THE CENTRAL VERMONT RAILWAY

Property damage was extensive when Train 444 derailed at East Alburg, only a short distance from the long trestle, on April 5, 1983. (Jim Murphy photo)

Southbound Train 560 is working State Line Hill near Monson, Massachusetts, on May 6, 1983. Six units are working this heavy train. (Robert Barnett photo)

THE CENTRAL VERMONT RAILWAY

The Duxbury Bridge, a popular rail photographer's site, is feeling the weight of five locomotives as they work Train 444 southward at 40 miles per hour on June 11, 1983. (Brian Irwin photo)

Northbound Train 447 is coming off the long pile trestle at East Alburg on June 30, 1983. Most of these cars are empties, bound for the Canadian National's Taschereau Yard in Montreal, some fifty miles away. (Tom Hildreth photo)

Crew caller Bobby Bean is at work in the call office located at St. Albans' Italy Yard in October 1983. The big board contains numbers of trains, on-duty times, and names of operating personnel—essential elements in properly staffing the road's trains. (Jim Murphy photo)

were moved to upper floors of buildings or taken by truck to Palmer. Windows were taped, and a freight train dropped off cuts of loaded cars on the wooden trestles between New London and Norwich in an effort to stabilize them against high winds and water.

Although damage was extensive in some communities, a combination of circumstances spared the railroad's property from heavy losses. Nonetheless, New London was without electrical power for six days, and so many trees were knocked down that one sectionman described the track between New London and Amherst as "eighty miles of cordwood."

During the year, part of the White River Junction roundhouse was leased to Northern Barns, a company specializing in the dismantling and reclamation of old barns in the region. The remainder of this once-busy rail facility was leased to Green Mountain Air Freight, a firm engaged in transporting air freight between Boston's Logan Airport and eastern Vermont.

In 1985, CV track forces installed thirteen thousand new ties, but no continuous welded rail was laid down. At the end of the year, the company operated 375 miles of track, and its equipment roster showed thirty locomotives and 226 freight cars. Three hundred employees were on the payroll.

For its year's efforts, the company earned a net income of $1.7 million, a significant turnaround from its half-million dollar loss the previous year. Although revenue figures for 1984 and 1985 were similar, the CV had been able to trim expenses by about $2 million in 1985. This major reduction in expenses was made possible by a minor reduction in personnel; through savings realized by faster release of cars unloaded on line; and by reductions in fuel consumption, personal injury claims, and joint-facility rental fees.

On January 1, 1986, all of the CV's data processing activities were organized into one department. This move was necessitated by the rapid growth of the role of the computer in the daily operations of the company. The CV acquired its

RS-11 No. 3608 leads smoke-belching sister Alcos across Central Street in Essex Junction on December 17, 1983. The southbound Train 444 is about to pass the Amtrak station just out of view at the left. (Alan Irwin photo)

first computer, an IBM System 32, to handle customer billing in 1977. By 1986, a System 38 was handling virtually all of the CV's financial activities, including payroll, general ledger, inventory, and interline freight accounting. Subsequently, the role of the computer was expanded into areas such as locomotive repair schedules and track and bridge repair and maintenance records.

Bombardier, Inc., a large Canadian-based manufacturer of light rail and conventional passenger equipment, operates a large manufacturing plant at Wilson Park in Websterville, Vermont. The new plant's first order was for 117 New Jersey Transit cars that were delivered in 1982–83. Served by the Washington County Railroad, cars going to and from the plant either for renovation or completion are interchanged with the CV at Montpelier Junction. Bombardier signed a $100 million contract with the New Jersey Transit Corporation in March 1986 for building twenty new cars and repairing and refurbishing 147 existing cars. Simultaneously, the manufacturer negotiated a $13 million, fifteen-car contract with Metro North Commuter Railroad.

Effective April 1, 1986, Amtrak started providing the personnel to operate its passenger trains. Several CV enginemen and conductors took personal leaves to operate the *Montrealer* between St. Albans and Springfield, Massachusetts, as Amtrak employees.

In mid-April, CV employees began a twenty-four-day work interruption because of picket lines established on CV property by a small number of Maine Central Railroad maintenance-of-way employees who had been striking their parent company, Guilford Transportation Industries, since March 3 over a job security issue. Union spokesman Vic Coffin stated that the CV was being pick-

The CV still hosted a local freight based at White River Junction in February 1984. The road's last Alco switcher, S-4 No. 8081, was normally assigned to this job. With a trace of Alco smoke and with fresh snow falling from the bridge over the White River south of Sharon, Vermont, the train made an impressive sight while returning to White River Junction after making a trip to South Royalton. (Fred G. Bailey photo)

eted because "our union alleges that the Central Vermont is aiding and abetting Guilford Transportation by moving freight that is Boston & Maine freight." (The B&M is a GTI railroad.)

When many of the CV's union workers refused to cross the picket line, about twenty-eight managers and supervisors operated some of the road's freight trains and provided other services necessary to keep the railroad running. When Amtrak employees refused to cross the picket lines, however, the passenger trains were canceled between Springfield, Massachusetts, and Montreal, and travelers were bused between these points.

Legal appeals by Central Vermont officials to district court judges in both Rutland and Washington to place a restraining order on the picketers brought "no-yes-no" responses as one decision after another was reversed. Picketers came and went at St. Albans, White River Junction, Brattleboro, Palmer, and New London, depending on the court order that was in effect on a given day.

In the meantime, other railroads connecting with GTI's Boston & Maine, Delaware & Hudson, and Maine Central were being seriously affected by this work interruption. The Vermont Railway, for example, was particularly hard hit—by late April more than forty of its employees had been laid off because of the severe decline in traffic. On April 24, the CV leased two Vermont Railway locomotives and hired one of its crews to handle the Burlington-St. Albans-White River Junction local freight work. Then, on April 29, with its freight business now cut in half, the CV began to hire about forty temporary workers to operate other trains and to provide ancillary services.

On Monday, May 5, Amtrak terminated its bus service between Montreal and Springfield, Massachusetts. At the same time, it announced that train service would be restored as soon as the labor issues had been settled. Although strike activities on CV property had been relatively peaceful, one incident of vandalism occurred at New London that was believed to be related to the strike. About eighty air hoses on freight cars had been cut and a number of coupler pins had been removed from cars and thrown away. Officials estimated that these damages totaled about $2,000.

After the strike spread across the country to Conrail and numerous other roads, President Reagan invoked the provisions of the Railway Labor Act on May 16. An emergency panel was created to meet during a sixty-day cooling off period, the pickets were taken down, and the strikers returned to work under pre-strike conditions. Acrimonious labor negotiations continued for the GTI employees, but the CV workers returned to their jobs and operations more or less returned to normal.

A northbound passenger extra crosses Chicopee Brook at North Monson, Massachusetts, on February 25, 1984. This 16-car special was sponsored by the Mass Bay Railroad Enthusiasts group, and it traveled from Boston to Brattleboro, Vermont, via New London, Connecticut. (Robert Barnett photo)

From high on a hillside in West Hartford, Vermont, we view a long train snaking its way northward across the White River about four miles north of White River Junction in March 1984. This was the site of the disastrous derailment, bridge collapse, and fire that claimed 30 lives and caused serious injuries to 37 others early on the morning of February 5, 1887. (Fred G. Bailey photo)

In early May, while the strike was in effect, the CV received its first long-awaited GP-38AC locomotive, Grand Trunk 5808. These units had proven themselves on many other roads, and CV personnel soon gave them high marks as well.

While the CV had realized some labor savings during the strike, increased per diem costs, legal fees incurred in the effort to remove pickets from CV property, and the cost of hiring contract workers combined to exceed the labor savings. In fact, the increased cost of operating trains during this labor dispute was a major factor in a 14 percent increase in operating expenses over 1985.

During the summer and fall of 1986, U.S. Sprint installed a fiber optics cable along the CV's 225-mile right of way from Palmer, Massachusetts, to East Alburg near the Canadian border. At that point, the cable was laid under Missisquoi Bay and then along the highway to Noyen, Quebec, where it was tied in with the Bell Canada system. Many CV employees were involved in this project, which progressed northward from Palmer at the rate of about twenty miles a week.

Grand Trunk No. 6253, an ex-Detroit, Toledo & Ironton two thousand-horsepower SD-38, pulled the trenching equipment. This unit, bedecked in a blue and orange paint scheme, was chosen for the job because it was equipped with a much-needed hump control. The fiber optics cable, which provides the clearest and fastest means of voice, video, and data transmission available, provided 144 channels for CV use. Although the CV committed $287,000 in capital funds over a two-year period to access this new system, railroad officials estimated the company would realize an annual decrease of $150,000 in its communications expenses as a result of accessing this new technology.

Commodities transported during the year included lumber (Sharon, VT; Belchertown and Palmer, MA; and South Windham, CT); newsprint (Norwich, CT; Monson and Palmer, MA); cement (Belchertown and Palmer, as well as Montpelier

36   THE CENTRAL VERMONT RAILWAY

S-4 No. 8081, the CV's last Alco switcher, is at work in the intermodal yard near Welden Street, St. Albans, on April 23, 1984. The 29-year-old locomotive was built in 1955 and was sold to K&L Feeds in Yantic, Connecticut, in early December 1987. (Alan Irwin photo)

The last southbound Rocket *is ready to leave the intermodal facility at St. Albans on May 3, 1984. GP-9 No. 4928 had the dubious distinction of handling this last train. (Alan Irwin photo)*

THE CENTRAL VERMONT RAILWAY 37

Jct., VT); and steel, gypsum products, plastics, and carbon dioxide (Palmer).

By the end of 1986, the CV was interchanging most of its bridge traffic with Conrail at Palmer rather than with the B&M at White River Junction. Traffic interchanged at Palmer increased by 4,200 carloads during the year, aided by the installation of a new crossover switch between the two roads. The traffic interchanged with the B&M at White River Junction, on the other hand, decreased by some seven thousand carloads from the 1985 level.

Although this increased length of haul increased both revenues and expenses, the result was a gain in net income for the CV. Overall, the company's income statement for 1986 showed a profit of $1.7 million, the same as in 1985. Revenue increased modestly from $21.1 million to $21.9 million, although the 38,600 cars handled represented a decline of about 5 percent from the previous year. It should be noted that the 1986 revenue figure included $1.6 million received from the fiber optic cable installation.

Competition from other carriers intensified in 1987. In particular, Conrail's success in attracting newsprint and other Canadian traffic to their route in New York State proved especially harmful to the CV.

Using regular freight service to move the New Jersey Transit cars between Harrison, New Jersey, and Bombardier's Websterville plant had proven to be too slow. As a result, Bombardier regularly incurred financial penalties for violations of the contracted time allowed for this work.

Fortunately, a meeting between the manufacturer and all interested parties produced a relatively simple solution: move the cars to and from Harrison via Amtrak's *Montrealer*—an overnight trip! The CV and Amtrak completed arrangements whereby the NJT cars would be dropped off and picked up at St. Albans. Special CV trains operated by two-man crews moved the cars between Montpelier Junction and St. Albans. The system was operated on a trial basis for several days, and it was found that transit time for these cars could be reduced from eleven to two days. Bombardier thereupon provided the CV with nine hundred car movements in 1987.

On April 6, 1987, Amtrak decided to cancel its *Montrealer* north of Springfield, Massachusetts, because of poor track conditions. The B&M's (Guil-

An 11-unit train on the CV (or on any other railroad, for that matter) was a rarity, and the fact that all units are lettered "CV" makes this assignment of power on Train 447 on May 5, 1984, particularly unusual. The northbound train is passing IBM's sprawling complex at Essex Junction. (Alan Irwin photo)

ford) trackage between Springfield and Windsor, Vermont, had deteriorated to the point where train speeds were reduced to ten miles per hour. Amtrak officials recognized that operating passenger trains at this speed would be unacceptable, so they decided to terminate the *Montrealer* at Springfield and provide bus service between that point and the Radisson Hotel in Burlington, Vermont. All Amtrak ticket offices in Vermont were closed except for White River Junction.

Not only did this poor trackage result in a loss to the CV of some $800,000 in passenger revenue per year, but it also greatly increased the cost of normal freight operations. Because of the time involved and the daily delays, eighteen locomotives rather than twelve were now required to power CV Trains 444 and 447. Extra crews were regularly needed, and fuel consumption was much higher than normal because of the inordinate amount of time required to get a train over the line. In addition, a number of costly derailments were directly attributable to the poor track conditions.

The forty-nine miles of track between Brattleboro and Windsor have long been used by both the CV and the B&M. For many years this trackage was the property of the B&M, with the Central Vermont having operating rights over it. After ongoing attempts by the CV to persuade the B&M to rehabilitate the line had failed, in late 1987 the CV joined with Amtrak and the State of Vermont in an effort to gain control of this section of track.

Meanwhile, for several years the CV's marketing personnel had worked to develop import-export business at the company's Long Pier in New London, Connecticut. These efforts paid off when Admiralty Group Limited leased the dock and adjacent storage facilities in 1987. The first ship to arrive tied up at the dock on July 26, flying the Danish flag and loaded with general cargo from Guyana, South America. Admiralty handles containerized cargo, which can be shipped to widespread markets by rail or truck. For the CV, in addition to revenue from the lease, the prospect of container traffic from Admiralty appeared favorable. This traffic was rather short-lived, however, and the warehouse was subsequently used for salt storage.

One of the CV's most unusual train movements in a long time occurred on August 2. When farmers in the Southeast suffered from one of the most devastating droughts in recent history, a call for

Several CV employees are participating in a safety class conducted at St. Albans by Amtrak personnel on May 16, 1984. (Jim Murphy photo)

As part of the railroad employees' ongoing training, several CV employees are receiving instruction from Amtrak personnel on firefighting. The large building in the background was built at Brattleboro as an enginehouse, but it was later dismantled and moved to Italy Yard in St. Albans, where it became the CV's car repair facility. (Jim Murphy photo)

help was issued. Several railroads, including the Central Vermont, responded to the emergency by transporting carloads of hay to the stricken farmers without charge.

In Vermont, Governor Madeleine Kunin and U.S. Representative James Jeffords surveyed the state and found many farmers were willing to donate bales of hay to their counterparts in the southeastern states. With that information, CV General Manager Phillip C. Larson offered to put the railroad in the hay-moving business.

From dawn until dusk on July 31 and August 1 farmers pulled up to railside locations with trucks and wagons loaded with bales of new hay. Volun-

Mechanical department employee Bob Yarger (in the hard hat) is chatting with visitor Bob Jones in the St. Albans enginehouse on June 2, 1984. (Jim Shaughnessy photo)

teer crews helped load the hay into boxcars, the doors of which were blocked open to allow the hay to continue drying while in transit. On August 2, a CV train manned by a volunteer crew and carrying a sizable complement of political, government, and railway people who had been involved with the project began its journey south from St. Albans. After adding hay-filled boxcars in Essex Junction, Montpelier Junction, Randolph, White River Junction, and Brattleboro, the train grew to seventy-two loaded cars before it left the state.

The train was turned over to Conrail at Palmer on the evening of August 2, which in turn interchanged the cars to Norfolk Southern at Alexandria, Virginia, for the remainder of the trip to Georgia. Farmers in the south were feeding Vermont hay to their livestock by August 5.

Vermont's Governor Madeleine Kunin presented the train crew with gifts of maple syrup during the stop at Montpelier Junction. Interestingly, each of these men—engineer Carlton Graves, conductor Paul Ladd, and brakeman Al Bruso—were farmers themselves, in addition to being veteran CV employees. Representative James Jeffords, who admitted to being a long-time railfan, was delighted with his first cab ride—and when engineer Graves offered to let him take the throttle, Jeffords jumped at the chance!

On August 21, as the southbound woodchip train was pulling out of the Oakland passing siding about five miles south of St. Albans, four cars derailed and 210 tons of woodchips spilled. Three of the four cars tipped over and sustained moderate damage, while about two hundred feet of track was torn up. Total damages were estimated to be about $80,000.

In late August, the first Canadian rail strike in fourteen years had an immediate and serious impact on CV operations. With most of its traffic

40   THE CENTRAL VERMONT RAILWAY

GP-9 No. 4926 is getting its nose lowered in the St. Albans backshop on June 2, 1984. Light and heavy locomotive repairs of all kinds were routinely handled by generations of workers in this St. Albans facility. (Jim Shaughnessy photo)

At the Springfield Terminal interchange at Charlestown, New Hampshire, CV Train 447 passes a B&M switcher and empty salt cars waiting to be picked up later in the day by a southbound B&M through freight. By this date, early June 1984, traffic was so infrequent on the original six-mile-long Springfield Terminal line over to Springfield, Vermont, that the B&M dropped off a locomotive and interchange cars whenever traffic for the ST showed up. (Fred G. Bailey photo)

THE CENTRAL VERMONT RAILWAY 41

coming through or from Canada, the curtailment of service by the Canadian National into St. Albans effectively shut off all incoming and outgoing traffic at this northern terminus. By August 24, approximately one-half of the road's 250 employees were laid off. Fortunately, however, the strike was of relatively short duration, and the CV workers were soon back on the job.

During the year, the Palmer office underwent a major renovation. Built in the 1860s, the building was once a freighthouse used for shipping and receiving large quantities of less-than-carload freight. However, since the mid-1960s, the structure had gradually become the nerve center for operations on the Southern Division. New partitions were added to create trainmaster's and roadmaster's offices, as well as a reception area, crew room, locker rooms, a shop area for carmen, a communication and signal center, and a general storage area. Soundproofing, new interior paneling, fresh paint, new signs, and landscaping gave the venerable structure a greatly improved appearance. In the fall, two additional tracks for use by mechanical and repair personnel were built at Palmer.

On October 21, a truck driver pulled his loaded propane tanker across the tracks at Vernon, Vermont, in front of the *Quasar,* the southbound Quaboag lumber train. Fortunately, the tank didn't rupture and a potential disaster was thus averted. The truck was pushed down the tracks for about thirty feet, and was then flipped off the track, landing upside down in a ditch. Miraculously, the driver escaped with relatively minor injuries. The lead locomotive, which was being operated by thirty-eight-year CV veteran Bobby Maynard, was damaged, and both the mainline and Vermont Route 142 were closed for the remainder of the day.

The CV started a popular Christmas tradition in 1978—the Northern Division's Santa Train. Each year this train was operated on a Saturday in mid-December for employees, their families, and the

CV through freight Train 444 is about to pass under a highway bridge near Northfield, Vermont, on June 16, 1984. The last Alco in this lash-up gives the impression that the fireman has just added new coal to the firebox! (Brian Irwin photo)

42   THE CENTRAL VERMONT RAILWAY

On June 29, 1984, normal operations on the Richford Branch came to a permanent end. The rear four cars of a combined Canadian Pacific-Boston & Maine detour train derailed at the east end of the long bridge spanning the Missisquoi River at Sheldon Junction. One car crashed through the east span of the bridge, and both the car and this section of the bridge were subsequently cut up. (Jim Murphy photo)

This view clearly shows some of the damage done to the equipment and bridge at Sheldon Junction by the 12:40 p.m. derailment on June 29, 1984. The bridge was never rebuilt and service was cut back to Sheldon Springs. (Jim Murphy photo)

public. Volunteer crews staffed the train, which usually consisted of four or five rented passenger cars and one or two CV cabooses. The trains operated from the St. Albans headquarters on Lake Street to various points on the mainline. Trips were run from 10:00 a.m. until 4:00 p.m., usually on an hourly basis. As the trains rolled along, Santa and his elves (all CV employees) walked through the cars passing out candy and small gifts to the children.

In 1986, this tradition spread to the Southern Division, where the trains operated out of Palmer. However, a shortage of staff and equipment caused these trips to be curtailed after three or four years.

At the end of 1987, the Central Vermont's income statement sadly revealed a net loss from the year's operations of $400,000, in sharp contrast to the $1.7 million net income figures posted in each of the two previous years. The major cause

(Top) *Amtrak's southbound* Montrealer *makes its scheduled stop at White River Junction on the night of July 4, 1984. Careful planning is necessary in order to get outstanding night shots such as this. (Leo Landry photo)*

(Above) *This equipment was virtually destroyed in the wreck of the* Montrealer *at Mile 106 south of Essex Junction on July 7, 1984. Five persons lost their lives when heavy rains and broken beaver dams undermined a culvert. This equipment was photographed ten days after the wreck as it was being assembled on the north end of the Richmond passing siding. (Leo Landry photo)*

(Right) *Jim Murphy was on hand on July 9, 1984, to photograph the track rebuilding effort and the removal of Amtrak No. 211 to the Richmond passing siding about three miles to the south.*

44   THE CENTRAL VERMONT RAILWAY

The Amtrak wreck in Williston on July 7, 1984, resulted in five deaths. This was the scene a couple of days later as the equipment is being removed and the track rebuilt. (Roger Wiberg photo)

The Amtrak equipment was pushed aside or removed to Richmond and the track was rebuilt within an arduous two-day period. This July 9, 1984, photograph shows Train 444, the first to pass through the wreck site. (Jim Murphy photo)

of this poor 1987 performance was attributed to a decrease of $1.9 million in revenue. While the number of carloads handled was about the same as in 1986, the revenue per car declined. This, in turn, was the result of an 18 percent decrease in the volume of high-revenue overhead traffic such as hazardous materials, chemicals, pulp and paper. The Canadian rail strike that began in late August was, at least in part, responsible for this decline in through traffic.

Gains were realized, however, from local traffic (that which originated and/or terminated on line). Woodchips loaded at Swanton and consigned to Burlington Electric's McNeil Generating Plant, as well as lumber handled by Quaboag Transfer's *Quasar* were the big gainers in this category. Also, traffic such as lumber, paper, and cement received from other railroads and off-loaded at various CV points showed a modest increase during the year.

A big disappointment occurred during the year when voters in Belchertown, Massachusetts, defeated a ballot item that would have allowed the CV to construct a large automobile distribution facility in that community. For nearly two years, the company had spent large amounts of time, effort, and money campaigning to get two-thirds of Belchertown's voters to change the zoning from agricultural to commercial on fifty-five of the 145 acres of land owned by the railroad. This change was necessary before the $8 million distribution terminal could be built.

Had this project been built, the Canadian National would have handled General Motors automobiles in covered cars from Sarnia, Ontario, to St. Albans, and the CV would have transported them to Belchertown. It was anticipated that this traffic would have amounted to about $20 million a year, doubling the road's current revenue. However, the voters' concerns over noise and increased traffic resulted in too many negative votes, and the CV was left with more than $1.1 million in expenses directly related to this effort.

Labor agreements were reached during the year with seven of the eleven unions that represented the CV employees, while the number of workers dropped from 294 to 269 during the period.

On the motive power front, numerous changes in the roster occurred in 1987. The CV leased five GP-9's from the Grand Trunk Western, while some aging RS-11's were taken out of service or returned to the parent company. The trackmen installed 3.0 miles of welded rail, somewhat less than the 5.1 miles that had been put down the previous year.

A major derailment occurred just before dawn on the morning of January 19, 1988, at the north switch at Fonda Junction, four miles north of St. Albans. Train 444 with one hundred cars was rolling southward from Montreal to St. Albans, manned by a Canadian National crew, when suddenly the brakes went into emergency. Initially, the crew suspected the train had broken apart, but when head brakeman Lee Pangborn (the author's cousin) made the long walk back to check things out, he found more than he had anticipated! Eighteen loaded cars were piled on top of each other, some standing on end in an adjacent pasture. Five of the cars carried grain, twelve carried lumber, and one contained newsprint.

The subsequent investigation indicated that the fiftieth car on the train had derailed at a switch, causing the pileup. One northbound train had to be canceled, as did a southbound train carrying woodchips from Swanton to the McNeil Generating Plant in Burlington. General manager Phil Larson estimated that damage to the eighteen cars would run between $30,000 and $80,000 each. He also noted that the CV's insurance had a high deductible, so in all likelihood the company would have to cover a significant amount of the repairs itself.

Hulcher Professional Services was called in to spearhead the cleanup effort, augmented by CV crews and personnel provided by Vermont Job Service. Several days of hard work were required to clear the track, salvage the spilled goods, and get the railroad operating again.

On February 1, 1988, the CV and the Lamoille Valley Railroad Corporation (LVRC) reached agreement on a plan that would allow LVRC trains to operate on CV trackage from Fonda Junction into Italy Yard in St. Albans and over 15.3 miles between Sheldon Junction and Richford. The latter trackage had been isolated from the rest of the CV's Richford Branch since the June 1984 derailment, which destroyed a section of the bridge at Sheldon Junction. This agreement allowed the LVRC to connect the CV mainline at Fonda Junction with Canadian Pacific tracks at Richford. However, after only a few months of operation,

46   THE CENTRAL VERMONT RAILWAY

The investigation of the July 7, 1984, wreck at Williston revealed that the Amtrak locomotive that day was not equipped with a radio frequency that could provide emergency weather bureau information. Thus, on July 16, 1984, little more than a week after the wreck, CN No. 2548 was used ahead of the Amtrak locomotive only for its radio. (Alan Irwin photo)

A heavy Train 444 is approaching Newton Road, St. Albans, on July 14, 1984. Canadian National and Central Vermont crews operated trains between St. Albans and Montreal on an equalized-mileage basis. Photographer Brian Irwin was two months short of his ninth birthday when he took this photograph!

THE CENTRAL VERMONT RAILWAY 47

The morning switcher crew poses in the locker room at Italy Yard for the camera of dispatcher Jim Murphy on July 18, 1984. Left to right are engineer Bud Roberts, brakeman Ken Barkyoumb, pin puller Paquette, conductor Howard Constantine (sitting), brakeman Lyle Jacobs, and yardmaster Don Kenyon.

In this pastoral scene, Train 444 skirts Mud Pond south of Roxbury, Vermont, in August 1984. The train has crested the line's ruling southbound grade, and the locomotive cab is now much quieter as the train is rolling downhill. (Roger Wiberg photo)

LVRC traffic west of its Morrisville headquarters virtually disappeared, and service into both St. Albans and Richford was terminated in March 1989.

Poor track conditions on the B&M's Conn River line south of White River Junction as well as Quaboag's difficulties in covering freight charges incurred in operating its intermodal lumber train, caused the CV to terminate the *Quasar* on February 7. The additional expenses and delays caused by the extremely slow speed limits on this trackage caused the train to regularly arrive late at Palmer, thus rendering the venture unprofitable. In addition, the train's late running interfered with other CV traffic.

In late June 1988, five loaded cars on Central Vermont Train 444 derailed at Westminster, Vermont, while traveling southbound at a speed of five miles per hour on the B&M's badly deteriorated trackage. One of the derailed cars contained liquid nitrogen, which began leaking. As a safety precaution, officials evacuated nearly one hundred people from their homes shortly after the 3:00 a.m. derailment. Fortunately, no personal injuries were sustained in the incident.

Meanwhile, Vermont Senator Patrick Leahy had been successful in pushing an amendment through Congress appropriating $5 million for the necessary track repairs on this line. Guilford, however, refused to allow any work to be started until a long-term contract had been negotiated with Amtrak covering usage of the track. Finally, after ten months of work by Senator Leahy to negotiate an agreement between Amtrak and Guilford went for naught, Amtrak announced in mid-February that it would request Guilford to sell the forty-nine-mile segment of its Conn River Line to the CV for $1 million. When this attempt failed, Amtrak petitioned the Interstate Commerce Commission to condemn the track and force the sale.

Finally, on August 5, 1988, the ICC's five-member panel authorized Amtrak to purchase this trackage for $2,373,286. As part of the ruling, Amtrak then immediately resold the property to the CV for the same price. Under this agreement, the Central Vermont acquired the right to manage and maintain the track for twenty years. Guilford was given the right to use the line for its freight trains during this period. This decision by the ICC freed up $5 million in federal money earmarked for the rehabilitation of the line.

It was a bit unusual to find a train of six units that were all lettered for the CV. Such is the case on this date as Train 554 makes its way through North Monson, Massachusetts. (Robert Barnett photo)

The CV's 700-series 2-10-4s are generally considered to have been the largest steam locomotives to operate in New England. However, they are not the largest steam locomotives to have traveled over CV rails. That distinction belongs to former Union Pacific 4-8-8-4 Big Boy No. 4012. When Steamtown, U.S.A. relocated from Bellows Falls to Scranton, Pennsylvania, the equipment moved over CV rails from Brattleboro to East Northfield, Massachusetts. The world's largest steam locomotive paused briefly at Brattleboro in November 1984 so Steamtown mechanical personnel could give it an inspection. It is being handled dead-in-tow in a B&M special train operating on the CV via trackage rights. (Fred G. Bailey photo)

GP-9 No. 4929 is ready to depart Italy Yard with a special move in 1984. The large building in the background is the Agway mill, an important CV customer. The large brick building in the right background is the ice house that for many years was used to supply refrigerator cars and passenger equipment with ice. The small frame structure that is partially visible at the left is the scale house. (Jim Murphy photo)

Winter has already arrived in Vermont, as southbound Train 444 passes the Suburban Gas siding about a mile north of Waterbury in December 1984. (Roger Wiberg photo)

Predictably, Guilford appealed this decision, claiming that the mandated sale price was only one-fourth of what the property was worth. The ICC eventually denied the appeal, however, and the sale was affirmed.

When the CV took control of this trackage at 7:00 a.m. on Saturday, September 10, a carefully developed rehabilitation plan was ready for execution. General manager Phil Larson had formed a team that included chief engineer Tom Faucett, manager of employee relations Jack Ovitt, engineer of communications and signals Ken Bagby, and Ty Gibson, who came to the CV in August as manager of operations. These men, as well as many other CV employees, spent hundreds of hours together working out the master plan and the myriad of details relating to this major rehabilitation effort.

In May, the CV hired Ray Duffany as project manager. He had served Conrail as a chief regional engineer, and subsequently had formed his own consulting firm in Florida. When Guilford officials would not permit the CV's engineering personnel onto the property to inspect it while negotiations were continuing with Amtrak and the CV, Duffany spent much time walking the track himself, mentally assessing what had to be done.

The challenge was to install fifty-four thousand ties, lay 6.5 miles of continuous welded rail, surface forty-nine miles of mainline and 6.5 miles of passing sidings, rebuild thirty-five private and ten public crossings, and rebuild dozens of turnouts. All of the work had to be done before the northern New England winter made completing the task impossible.

Amtrak and Grand Trunk Corporation sent sophisticated track equipment from various places around the country to supplement CV's maintenance-of-way equipment, and these machines were marshaled at Brattleboro. Workers arrived from all over the country—many came from other railroads and from as far away as Florida, Texas, and Washington. Some were experienced workers furloughed from other roads, while others had no previous railroad experience.

With the approval of the Federal Railroad Administration, the existing CTC system was deacti-

The Burlington-bound woodchip train is kicking up clouds of light snow as it rolls through Colchester Station at 40 miles per hour on January 26, 1985. It takes only about two hours to unload 20 or 21 of these 7,000-cubic-foot hopper cars at the Burlington Electric Company's generating plant. The cars will then be returned to St. Albans and subsequently respotted at the loading facility at East Swanton. (Brian Irwin photo)

vated, and the line began operating under manual block system (MBS) rules. It was intended that MBS would control all movements over the line until a new CTC dispatcher's board could be installed at St. Albans. Work began on September 14. Everyone involved in the project spent the morning at the Putney Inn, where an intensive session of safety lectures, rules review, and discussions of the task at hand prepared the workers for their assignment. In the afternoon, the men were assigned to their jobs and new recruits were given an opportunity to familiarize themselves with the tools and machinery they would be using. Wages ranged from $7.90 to $14.00 per hour, depending on the workers' experience and the skills required for the job. The CV secured living accommodations for the workers at area motels, not an easy task when every room in the state is booked by leaf-peepers at this time of the year.

The work progressed very well during the ensuing weeks. In fact, the tie-replacement phase that was scheduled to be finished by December 6 was completed just before Thanksgiving. The 6.5 miles of continuous welded rail was installed at the north end of the job, the ballasting (fifteen thousand tons of stone) was completed, and the whole rehabilitation project was wrapped up ahead of schedule. Perhaps most significant of all was the fact that only $3.2 million of the $5 million appropriation was spent.

The Golden Spike Ceremony commemorating the completion of the work was held at Windsor in front of the former passenger station on Tuesday, December 21. Central Vermont GP-9 4559, which had been named "George J. Harmon" the previous year to honor the CV's late chief mechanical officer, and caboose 4909 departed St. Albans for Windsor at 8:30 a.m. with CV president Gerald Maas, general manager Phil Larson, and other officials on board. Unaffected by a severe ice storm that had made many of the state's highways impassable, the trip was made at the passenger train speed of fifty-nine miles per hour.

A stop was made at Middlesex, four miles from Senator Leahy's home, to pick up the senator, his wife, and his daughter. Leahy rode in the cab of locomotive 4559, and upon the train's arrival in Windsor, he excitedly told the waiting crowd that

In a way, this beautiful February 1985 winter scene marks the beginning of the decline of the CV. The lead unit, No. 4926, had just been rebuilt in the St. Albans shop with a chopped nose, and it was the next-to-the-last rebuild to be done at St. Albans. The traffic volume had already begun to slip, and within one year blue-and-orange Grand Trunk power began arriving, signaling the end of the CV's local paint schemes. (Alan Irwin photo)

52   THE CENTRAL VERMONT RAILWAY

On a cold February 2, 1985, the Burlington woodchip train makes it way across an interesting trestle near Colchester behind GP-9's Nos. 3612 and 3606. The latter unit was sold to Quaboag Transfer nine months after this photo was taken by Alan Irwin.

The woodchip cars are being unloaded at the Burlington Electric Department's plant located on the Intervale at Burlington on February 2, 1985. The unusually large size of these cars becomes evident when one contrasts them with the size of the locomotives. (Alan Irwin photo)

THE CENTRAL VERMONT RAILWAY

he had "just realized every kid's (and forty-eight-year-old man's) dream of driving a locomotive."

Earlier in the day, crews posed GP-38 No. 5808 and Amtrak F40PH No. 401 nose to nose, about thirty feet apart. The front platform of the 5808 served as a podium for Senator Leahy and other officials. When the speakers made little progress in driving home a gold-painted spike with a similarly finished maul, foreman Ron Boucher took the maul and completed the task in an experienced, professional manner.

Referring to his less-than-sterling performance with the spike maul in front of sixty smiling track workers, Senator Leahy explained: "It's not as easy as it looks. That's why I work in the Senate and not for the railroad." Then, after being offered the use of a stretch limousine for the return trip to Middlesex, the senator declined in favor of the locomotive cab again. "I can ride in a limousine any day," he said.

The rehabilitated track was now good for freight train speeds of forty miles per hour, while passenger trains were allowed to travel at fifty-nine miles per hour. CV dispatcher Jim Murphy raised an interesting point when he noted that the dispatchers had planned train movements and meets based on speeds of five and ten miles per hour over this forty-nine-mile section of track for so long that they would now have to make across-the-board adjustments in their planning in order to accommodate the faster speeds. It was, he said, "like working on another railroad."

In October 1988, the United Transportation Union (UTU) settled a contract that gave the CV increased flexibility in the use of train crews. It also provided for the elimination of firemen and the operation of some trains with two-man crews. In addition, an agreement with the Transportation Communications Union (TCU) gave workers in other crafts the authority to utilize computer terminals, thus eliminating the need for TCU clerks at several locations.

On the Southern Division, all supervisory and clerical functions formerly performed at New London, Connecticut, were consolidated at Palmer. These changes were meant to reduce operating

(continued on page 72)

Five CN road units bring a heavy Train 444 across the long East Alburg drawbridge on May 11, 1985. All trains must stop before moving onto the structure, and the maximum speed over the trestle is ten miles per hour. The building is used by the drawtender during the summer and early fall months. (Jim Shaughnessy photo)

The freshly painted GT 3604 emerges from the St. Albans paint shop on July 14, 1979. The painter was touching up the yellow only moments before Ed Betz took this rare photo. Within a few days, the "GT" lettering was replaced by "CV." At this time, the locomotive was awaiting a main generator and was out of service. No. 3604 was sold to Genesee Valley Leasing Company in June 1988. The new owner converted the "CV" into "GV" by modifying the "C." (Courtesy Alan Irwin)

This southbound rail train was photographed at South Willington, Connecticut, on August 28, 1981, by Robert Barnett. The installation of continuous welded rail was an ongoing program over the years, and by the early 1990s approximately half of the CV's mainline trackage had been upgraded.

This view of the lower portion of the CV's yard at New London was taken from the I-95 overpass in July 1982. The busy bay and Long Island Sound may be seen in the distance. (Leo Landry photo)

Leo Landry captured two GP-9's (Phase II) at Brattleboro on the night of August 6, 1982. No. 4549 was the last unaltered original CV GP-9 when it went to the Grand Trunk Western in September 1990. No. 4551 went to the GTW a year earlier. Both units were built in March 1957.

This shippers' special was operated by the CV and the B&M to promote the recently expanded intermodal service to Springfield, Massachusetts, and New Haven, Connecticut. The train had both CV and B&M motive power, Maine Central (GTI) coaches, and observation car "Sam Pinsly." The latter was an ex-B&O, ex-StJ&LC car owned by Mr. Pinsly's daughter, Mrs. Maggie Silver. (Alan Irwin photo)

57

The Middle River winds through downtown Stafford Springs, Connecticut, and here it provides an attractive setting for northbound local freight Train 561 on May 6, 1983. (Robert Barnett photo)

In 1984, general manager Phil Larson made it known that he wanted a CV company Christmas card that "looked like a Howard Fogg painting." To meet the request, photographer Alan Irwin set up this scene well in advance of Train 444's passing through Milton on January 15, 1984. As the terrain in this area is not conducive to sliding, the sleds were merely props. By prior arrangement, engineer George Gay waved at just the right time. (Alan Irwin photo)

CV Train 447 is working its way northward through the Winooski River valley on a beautiful spring day in 1985. The train is between Middlesex and Waterbury, Vermont, at a locale known as "Slip Hill." (Gary Knapp photo)

Train 556's three units are working the Amherst College coal storage track on August 13, 1985. Note the transposition of numbers on one of 4926's number boards. (Robert Barnett photo)

59

The CV sold Nos. 3611 and 3606 to Quaboag Transfer to provide the power for that company's Quasar *piggyback trains. The two RS-11's were freshly painted in an automotive metallic green color for this service that began operating over the CV on November 17, 1985. This same paint was used on QT's fleet of trucks. The logo on the locomotives includes a truck—perhaps the only railroad logo that does so. No. 3611 suffered an engine explosion on October 6, 1986, and it never ran again. (Alan Irwin photo)*

A southbound local freight is going under U.S. Route 7 south of St. Albans on April 3, 1986. VTR No. 801 was on a two-week lease to the CV. The subway cars are being taken to Montpelier Junction for interchange to the Washington County Railroad, which will deliver them to the Bombardier plant in Barre for finishing. CV No. 3608 was a one-of-a-kind RS-11 that was rebuilt by the Duluth, Winnipeg & Pacific at its Virginia, Minnesota, shops. (Alan Irwin photo)

60

The power is tied down after a minor derailment at Belchertown, Massachusetts, on May 2, 1986. The southbound train's lead unit is Vermont Railway No. 801, which was on a short-term lease to the CV. (Robert Barnett photo)

With a Quaboag Transfer unit leading, Extra 3611 North rumbles through Three Rivers, Massachusetts, on May 10, 1986. The Ware and Quaboag rivers merge and become the Chicopee River at this point. (Robert Barnett photo)

This impressive display of motive power is working Train 447 near Charlestown, New Hampshire, on April 25, 1986. The Boston & Maine was on strike, and abnormal operations resulted for the other railroads in the region. These twelve units,

several of which were being shuttled back to St. Albans, were leader CV 4928, followed by CV 4447, CN 2575, CV 4549, CN 2579, CV 4550, CV 4548, leased VTR 801, and CV units 3612, 3608, 4929, and 4925. (Leo Landry photo)

CV 4551 leads a five-unit lash-up and Train 447 north over the Sugar River Bridge near Claremont, New Hampshire, on June 14, 1986. (Ken Houghton photo)

For a couple of months during the summer of 1986, the Quasar *left St. Albans shortly after dawn, thereby opening up many new photo possibilities for railfans. This train is skirting glass-like Mud Pond, Roxbury, mid-morning on June 15, 1986, before the hot summer sun caused wind currents that often rippled the water. (Alan Irwin photo)*

This rare assemblage of motive power—CV 8081, Clarendon & Pittsford 752, Green Mountain 401, and CV 4929—pose at Palmer in July 1986 while on their way to Braintree, Massachusetts, where they were featured at the Railroad Enthusiasts (Mass Bay) Convention. (Richard C. Barnett photo)

Train 562 is setting out cars at State Line (Massachusetts) in July 1986. These cars will be picked up by Train 555, the turn job from New London, to be delivered to Southern Division customers. (Richard C. Barnett photo)

65

Quaboag Transfer RS-11's 3611 and 3606 are working southbound piggyback Train 244 alongside the Boston & Maine's double-track line near Miller Falls, Massachusetts, on June 26, 1986. (Robert Barnett photo)

This view shows some of the equipment that was used to lay the Sprint fiber optics cable the entire length of the CV mainline from Connecticut to the U.S.-Canadian border. Stephen D. Carlson took this photo at Millers Falls, Massachusetts, on July 31, 1986.

Monson, Massachusetts, is the setting for this photograph of Train 444 that was taken by Bill Gleason on November 23, 1986. Chop-nosed GP-9 No. 4926 is leading five other units assigned to this heavy Southern Division train. (Ken Houghton collection)

CV No. 3608 posed with No. 4559 in bright sunlight in front of the St. Albans locomotive shop on May 3, 1987. When the CV's rebuild program was augmented to include a chop-nose unit, measurements were taken of the nose of the 3608. The yellow-nose modification of the so-called Mumley green paint scheme was done by retaining the green between the two yellow strips and painting everything else yellow. (Alan Irwin photo)

GP-9 No. 4558 is leading Train 447 across the diamond at Bellows Falls on August 4, 1987. The other trackage in this photograph belongs to the Green Mountain Railroad. The rear of the GMRC's Green Mountain Flyer *passenger train is visible at the right. The passenger depot, now owned by the GMRC, is behind the locomotives. This facility is used by two daily Amtrak trains as well as the Green Mountain Railroad's seasonal passenger trains. (Leo Landry photo)*

Train 444, with GP-9 No. 4559 in the lead, has caught the attention of a farmer as it passes his hayfield near Waterbury, Vermont, on August 8, 1987. Through the years many large and prosperous dairy farms operated along the CV's route. (Gary Knapp photo)

68

The rear of Train 444 is still in Italy Yard as the head end of the long southbound train passes the CV's general office building in St. Albans in March 1988. These trains typically ran 100 or more cars, requiring a minimum of six units to make the climb to Roxbury. (Gary Knapp photo)

A southbound passenger extra is on the south end of the passing siding at Oakland, about five miles south of St. Albans, for a meet with Train 447. Gary Knapp took this photo on April 12, 1988.

69

Power from Train 323 is being serviced at the St. Albans engine terminal on June 11, 1988. Most of these GP-38AC's had arrived on the property only four months earlier. (Jim Shaughnessy photo)

No. 5808, in fresh paint, is teamed with GP-9 No. 4559 to lift the Burlington wayfreight up the grade out of St. Albans. On days when the twenty woodchip cars were in the consist, two units were needed on the head end. This photo was taken by Alan Irwin from the Route 7 overpass about two miles south of town.

70

Large quantities of lumber are being loaded at the intermodal facility at St. Albans in the mid-1980s. This small yard was very busy for an all-too-brief period of time in the history of the CV. (Jim Murphy photo)

Train 444 is passing the Swanton station on May 11, 1985, and a hard eight-mile climb to Italy Yard lies ahead. Swanton's rail customers were served daily by switchers operating out of Italy Yard. (Jim Shaughnessy photo)

costs and to improve service to customers. To these ends, another six miles of welded rail were installed in Connecticut during the year.

Revenues in 1988 totaled $22.5 million, an increase of $2.5 million over the previous year. This gain was the result of rate increases as well as a growth in the percentage of traffic terminating on the line. Unfortunately, however, expenses rose from $21.9 million to $23.4 million, primarily from inordinately high operating costs on the Windsor-Brattleboro section prior to its rehabilitation. The CV's operating loss of $900,000 was still about $1 million better than the company's 1987 performance.

Conrail continued to be the CV's strongest rail competitor, and a considerable amount of long-haul traffic was lost during the year to the bigger road because it was able to undercut the CV's rates on various commodities.

The majority of the road's traffic continued to be received from parent Canadian National, and in 1988 60 percent of this traffic terminated on the CV. During the year, fourteen new customers were added along the line—consignees for incoming shipments of cement, plastics, liquid gases, woodpulp, and fuel oil. Some growth also occurred at various existing distribution facilities involving lumber, newsprint, and cement. Most of this growth occurred on the Southern Division, as the Northern Division now had only about a dozen active customers.

One of these customers was PMI Lumber Transfer, which leased the CV's ten-acre industrial site at Sharon, Vermont. Before the year was over, nearly two thousand cars of lumber were unloaded at this facility. This property had formerly been leased by Canfor USA Corporation for lumber distribution throughout northern New England. PMI also leased the former Weyerhaeuser warehouse in Royalton, Vermont, where an additional five hundred carloads of plywood were handled during the year.

Shortly before noon on Friday, March 31, 1989, the second, third, and fourth cars of Train 447

Alco RS-11's were photographed in the dead line at St. Albans by Jim Shaughnessy on May 11, 1985. Seen here are Nos. 3614, 3602, 3610, 3603, 3608, 3609, 3611, 3613, and 3607. These units were eventually sold or scrapped, some within weeks of this photograph. At this time, S-4 No. 8081 and RS-11's Nos. 3606 and 3612 were stored serviceable at the St. Albans enginehouse.

72   THE CENTRAL VERMONT RAILWAY

We are looking west as Train 550 has been spotted for unloading at the Burlington Electric Department's generating plant. The locomotives have been run around the train and are now on the north end for the trip back to St. Albans. (Jim Shaughnessy photo)

The woodchip train is on its way back to St. Albans on May 11, 1985. Here it is leaving the eight-mile Burlington Branch at Essex Junction as the engineer blows for the busy Maple Street crossing. (Jim Shaughnessy photo)

The train on the left is standing on the freight main, Track 101, in Italy Yard. SW-1200 switchers Nos. 1511 and 1509 were normally used together as the combined horsepower was necessary to break apart and switch out the heavy trains. In this May 11, 1985, photo, they are putting together a northbound train on the upper side of the yard. (Jim Shaughnessy photo)

Northbound Train 447 skirts the Connecticut River just north of North Walpole, New Hampshire, on May 17, 1985. The track to the left is an 8,887-foot passing siding. (Leo Landry photo)

derailed in Vernon. A covered hopper, the second car on the train, remained upright. However, the next car, a CV tankcar, rolled onto its side, blocking an adjacent track. A boxcar immediately behind the overturned tank car also remained upright. The scene was cleared in short order, and the interruption in service was minimal.

In June, Amtrak worked out an agreement with the unions representing the Canadian National employees who operate trains between Montreal and St. Albans. Immediately upon the conclusion of these negotiations, Amtrak spokesman Clifford Black announced that the *Montrealer* would resume service between Montreal and Washington, through Vermont, on July 18, 1989.

Although Amtrak officials remained interested in operating these trains over the former route through Springfield, Massachusetts, this was not feasible until fifty miles of track in Massachusetts was upgraded similar to the work recently completed in Vermont. Instead, a new route would now take the *Montrealer* all the way to New London on CV tracks, with stops at Amherst, Massachusetts, and Willimantic, Connecticut. Amtrak also announced that it would continue to offer its daily *Yankee Clipper* and *Connecticut Yankee* bus service between Burlington, Vermont, and Springfield, Massachusetts.

A northbound Amtrak train rolled over the route on July 17 carrying railroad, government, and Amtrak officials, and other invited guests. Stops were made at the communities that would be served, and at each stop the train was greeted by enthusiastic crowds of people, many of them displaying banners and carrying signs of welcome. Those on board were given a variety of souvenirs commemorating the return of passenger service on the CV.

Dignitaries vied for room in the locomotive cab at each stop. At Bellows Falls, Vermont's Governor Madeleine Kunin and Senator Patrick Leahy climbed into the cab. As the governor settled into the engineer's seat, she looked down at the crowd, shrugged her shoulders, and asked, "What do I do

This impressive aerial photograph shows a seven-unit southbound train led by GP-9 4550 crossing the Connecticut River at East Northfield, Massachusetts, on May 25, 1985. (Ken Houghton photo)

now?" This equipment continued on to Montreal, where the following day it became the consist of the first southbound *Montrealer* to operate since early April 1987.

In late August 1989, a new customer commenced operations at Windsor, utilizing twenty thousand square feet of the old Goodyear plant. The newly formed Windsor Distribution Terminal, owned by Neil Richardson and his wife Mickie, started receiving wood pulp in boxcars for distribution to paper mills in New Hampshire via truck.

After serving as general manager of the CV for twelve years, on October 5, 1989, Phillip C. Larson announced his resignation "to pursue other interests." Larson, who had come to the CV as a seasoned railroader in 1977, was generally regarded as a very active, hands-on official. Gerald L. Maas, president of the CV's parent Grand Trunk Corporation, said in a news release that Phil Larson "has been a valuable member of the Grand Trunk Corporation, and we will miss his experience and expertise." Maas credited Larson with guiding the CV "through the competitive challenges spurred by deregulation and the changing economic conditions of the Northeast."

A successor was not immediately named, but in early November president Maas announced that Larson would be succeeded by Christopher J. Burger, effective December 1. The new general manager came to the CV after twenty-two years on the Chicago and Northwestern Railroad, where he had capably filled a variety of roles, including division superintendent and assistant vice president—transportation.

GP-18 No. 3614 and GP-9 No. 4926 are undergoing repairs in the backshop at the St. Albans enginehouse on June 18, 1985. Tools, equipment, and supplies common to this type of facility are much in evidence in this impressive photograph. (Alan Irwin photo)

Train 562 is working through the south end of the CV's yard at Amherst, Massachusetts on July 23, 1985. Three GP-9's are providing the power on this day. (Robert Barnett photo)

This photograph of the CV's only two GP-18's was taken in Italy Yard on September 1, 1985. The road's second No. 3602 and the second No. 3614 were both ex-Rock Island units. Both were sold to the Grand Trunk Western on September 3, 1991, and both subsequently went to the Georgia Central six months later. (Alan Irwin photo)

GP-9 No. 4551 handles a special southbound movement past the Amherst passenger station on October 27, 1985. (Robert Barnett photo)

Locomotives 4925 and 4926 were photographed at Palmer, Massachusetts, on December 15, 1985. No. 4925 still wears white number boards from its days in the "Battle Creek Blue" paint that was erroneously applied at the Battle Creek shops. (Dan Foley photo, courtesy Alan Irwin)

During the 1986 strike, Vermont Railway locomotives and personnel were used to operate trains in and out of St. Albans. A VTR GP-38 and SW-1500 are working a northbound train over the Georgia High Bridge on April 24, 1986. (Bonnie Irwin photo)

In early October, the CV was cited by the EPA for dumping oil and wastewater into a small brook that runs through the St. Albans engine terminal on its way to Lake Champlain. These charges resulted in a lawsuit being filed against the railroad in Superior Court. CV spokesperson Rosalyn Graham described the situation as one of "bad housekeeping" and indicated that the company would contest the citation and any subsequent fines. At the same time, the Vermont attorney general's office also filed suit against the railroad for alleged violations of the state's air pollution, waste management, and water pollution laws.

During the year, law enforcement officers and media people had an opportunity to see first-hand what locomotive crews encounter at grade crossings on virtually every trip. This Operation Lifesaver project, which was called "Trooper on the Train," took place on May 4. It was designed to impress on drivers the importance of obeying crossing signals and not taking chances.

With police officers and media representatives aboard the lead engine of a southbound freight train, drivers of vehicles that ran the crossing signals were reported to other officers stationed nearby. They, in turn, stopped the vehicles and issued citations to the offending drivers. This first trip targeted four crossings in St. Albans, three in Milton, two in Colchester, and four in Essex Junction. Subsequently, other areas were brought under similar surveillance.

During the year, the sale of unneeded property in New London netted the CV approximately $1 million dollars of much needed income. Six more miles of continuous welded rail was installed at various locations, and a major resurfacing project was also completed. Several furloughed trackmen were recalled to handle this work. Also, a computer-assisted manual block system developed by the Canadian National Railway was made operational.

Through the efforts of the CV's marketing personnel, a new gateway to the CSX Corporation was established via the Green Mountain Railroad at Bellows Falls (North Walpole), the Vermont Railway, and the Delaware & Hudson. One of the primary commodities using this route was flyash moving from Montville, Connecticut, to Virginia and West Virginia. An average of more than sixty carloads of this material began moving over the road in open hoppers each week.

CV Train 562 is picking up a long cut of cars from Conrail at Palmer on May 4, 1986. Six units, Nos. 4448, 4450, 4924, 4923, 3614, and 3602, are on the job this day. The old Boston & Albany freight house is on the left. (Robert Barnett photo)

80 THE CENTRAL VERMONT RAILWAY

Vermont Railway power and crew are bringing a local freight past the CV's general office building on May 7, 1986, during the strike. A striking employee's automobile is parked at the left. (Alan Irwin photo)

With white flags flying, Train 444 rolls past a piggyback train at the intermodal yard in St. Albans on April 27, 1986. The CV's Bob Harmon (on the left) talks with Jack Bliss, while Quaboag president Kirk Bryant stands at the cab door of RS-11 No. 3608. (Alan Irwin photo)

Total carloads handled by the CV during 1989 decreased by nearly 9 percent from the previous year. A decline in construction activity in New England resulted in fewer carloads of lumber and cement being handled. The Canadian newsprint traffic also was down. From rail operations, the company suffered an alarming $3.7 million loss. When income from the sale of real estate was factored in, the company's net loss for the year stood at $1.7 million.

The decade of the 1980s had not been good to the CV. During this ten-year period, the number of carloads handled decreased nearly 40 percent—from fifty-seven thousand in 1980 to thirty-five thousand in 1989. Over the years, the company's operating losses often had been at least partially offset by the sale of real estate and by infusions of cash by parent Canadian National. Employee and official alike, however, realized that eventually there would be no more real estate to sell and that the parent company, which was having serious financial problems of its own, would decline further financial support.

Since the middle of the nineteenth century, the Central Vermont had owned a considerable amount of land on Burlington's Lake Champlain waterfront. A good portion of this acreage represented fill that had pushed back the original marshy shoreline nearly 150 years ago. The CV's rail yard and other facilities at this location had become redundant, and its needs could now be met by a single track with which to gain access to the nearby Vermont Railway yard for the interchange of cars. Now perhaps the most valuable acreage in the county (if not in the state), it has been coveted for several years by commercial developers as well as by the City of Burlington and the State of Vermont. In fact, this land had been the subject of legal controversy since 1984, when the railroad and the city went to court to obtain a ruling on its ownership. The following year, the Chittenden Superior Court ruled that the Central Vermont had a legal title to the land, but that it must be put to "public use." The CV immediately appealed the decision.

Extra 4551 North (Train 447) is passing a picturesque covered bridge near Hartland, Vermont, on June 14, 1986. This scene is adjacent to the northbound lanes of Interstate 91. (Ken Houghton photo)

Train 562, the Palmer Local, returns to the small but busy Palmer Yard after handling some on-line switching chores in July 1986. Train 444's mixture of CN and CV power was being used for this move. (Richard C. Barnett photo)

The conductor on southbound intermodal Train 244 has extinguished a traction motor fire on Quaboag Transfer RS-11 No. 3611 near Barretts, Massachusetts, on July 22, 1986. The nearby Belchertown Fire Department was summoned to cool down the equipment. (Robert Barnett photo)

This train is in the process of laying a Sprint fiber optic cable between Palmer, Massachusetts, and the Canadian border along the CV's right-of-way. Jim Murphy photographed the northbound train at Mud Pond, south of Roxbury, Vermont, in September 1986. Specially equipped Grand Trunk SD-38 No. 6253 was the regular power on this job.

In 1985, the Alden Corporation put together a $100 million proposal for the development of the property. Burlington voters, however, defeated a $6 million bond issue that was an integral part of the proposal, and the Alden plan quickly faded into oblivion.

In late 1988, the CV proposed a $170 million master plan for commercial and residential use of thirty-two acres of this land. The plan included a hotel, a restaurant, condominiums and apartments, offices, stores, and two marinas. It was not well received, however, despite a variety of benefits to both the public and private sectors that the CV claimed for the proposal.

Meanwhile, attorneys for the City of Burlington countered the CV's proposal by arguing that the public trust doctrine should be applied to the case. This legal philosophy dictates that the state should be named as guardian of a waterfront property in order to protect the shoreline from private development and for the public good.

The issue was taken to the Vermont Supreme Court, which ruled on December 22, 1989, that the Central Vermont could not develop this land

Train 447 is pulling across Lake Street in St. Albans on a summer day in 1986. A St. Albans Messenger photographer stood on the balcony of the general office building to take this unique photograph. (St. Albans Messenger photo, courtesy Jim Murphy)

To assist drought-stricken farmers in the southeastern United States, their counterparts in Vermont and other northern states cut and loaded many carloads of hay, which were shipped south late in the summer of 1986. A trainload of hay is passing through Essex Junction on August 2, 1986, as Senator Jim Jeffords, CV general manager Phil Larson, and an official from the Vermont Agricultural Commission stand outside the cab of No. 4926. (Alan Irwin photo)

An immaculate chop-nosed GP-9 No. 4926 has just brought a directors' special into Brattleboro on October 7, 1986. The two-car train has stopped in front of the passenger depot. (Robert Barnett photo)

86   THE CENTRAL VERMONT RAILWAY

The northbound Montrealer *blasts across North Williston Road, about 28 miles south of St. Albans, at 59 miles per hour (the maximum allowed in non-signaled territory) in December 1986. Photographer Alan Irwin, with his hood up and poised for a quick turn, took this photograph with a 210 mm lens to minimize the danger caused by pieces of ice flying from the snowbank.*

(Right) *This beautiful photo of Train 444 was taken near Monson, Massachusetts, four days before Christmas in 1986. Train crews generally preferred to operate the locomotives short hood leading because of improved visibility. (Ken Houghton photo)*

because title to the property was valid only as long as it was used for railroad purposes, wharfing, or warehousing. Thus, if the CV attempted to develop the property for other uses, the state could reclaim the shoreline under the public trust doctrine.

The Central Vermont appealed this decision to the U. S. Supreme Court in March 1990, but in May the appeal was rejected. Meanwhile, the state legislature decided that a ten-acre park and an eight hundred-foot shoreline promenade the city wanted to build would be a suitable use of some of this property. Burlington voters, meanwhile, had approved a $2 million bond for lakefront development in 1988. However, nothing could be done with the property until the railroad and the city could agree on a price for the land and resolve various other differences.

On June 8, after numerous rounds of public meetings and a twelve-hour secret session, an agreement was finally reached whereby the City

(Above) *Rolling northward through the snow-covered Green Mountains at 60 miles per hour, Amtrak's Montrealer is running a bit late on the morning of January 24, 1987. Camels Hump, one of the state's highest peaks, provides the backdrop for this dramatic view of winter railroading. (Alan Irwin photo)*

(Left) *A southbound train headed by 30-year-old GP-9 No. 4917 works its way between Monson and State Line on the CV's Southern Division on April 26, 1987. (Ken Houghton photo)*

of Burlington would purchase 8.5 acres to be used for a park for $500,000. In addition, the city was granted a twelve-month option to purchase another forty-five acres, most of which is located north of the defunct Moran Generating Plant, at a price to be negotiated. The agreement allowed the CV to keep a sixty-foot right of way along the eastern side of the 8.5-acre section, and the city would pay all track relocation costs.

In other matters, the CV's newly reorganized Transportation Center was relocated from the yard office at Italy Yard to the main floor of the general

Six CV locomotives are taking Train 447 across the Georgia High Bridge, ten miles south of St. Albans, on a beautiful late summer day in 1987. (Gary Knapp photo)

The lumber cars on the head end of this five-unit Train 444 will be set off at Sharon, Vermont. The train is crossing the much photographed bridge at Duxbury, within sight of passing motorists on I-89 and Route 100, on August 8, 1987. (Gary Knapp photo)

RS-11 No. 3606 was leased by the CV to Quaboag Transfer for use on their "Quasar" train in November 1985. This unit was built by Alco in 1956 and was later sold to the Winchester & Western in October 1988. No. 3608 was sold to the Lamoille Valley Railroad in March 1988. White River Junction was the location of this night shot by Leo Landry.

(Left) CV freight Train 444 is climbing the grade at Roxbury on August 14, 1987. This photo was taken from the Rabbit Hollow Bridge located about one mile north of the crest of the long grade. (Alan Irwin photo)

office building on Lake Street in April. Personnel involved in this move included train dispatchers and those working in the car control and customer service center. Upon the completion of this relocation, the Italy Yard building was closed and made available for sale or lease.

The CV led all seventeen U.S. railroads that handled Amtrak trains in on-time performance of these trains during the five-month period of April through August 1990. The CV's contract with Amtrak provided a monetary incentive for on-time handling, so in addition to the pride factor, this performance put money in the railroad's bank account.

On May 7, the last piece of ninety-pound rail on the CV's mainline was removed at Stafford, Connecticut. Two days later, the last piece of eighty-five-pound rail also was removed, some of

As the Burlington-bound woodchip train was pulling out of the Oakland passing siding about five miles south of St. Albans on August 21, 1987, four loaded cars derailed. Three of the four cars overturned, 210 tons of chips were spilled, and 200 feet of track had to be rebuilt. (Jim Murphy photo)

Train 447 has just crossed Brigham Road at the north end of Italy Yard in St. Albans on October 16, 1987. Most of the cars on this typically long train are empties bound for Montreal. (Jim Shaughnessy photo)

The CV's sole Alco S-4 was sold to K&L Feeds in Yantic, Connecticut, for use as a plant switcher in late 1987. The 32-year-old locomotive was given a new paint job at the St. Albans shops and was photographed on December 4, 1987, on its way to begin service for its new owner. (Jim Murphy photo)

which had been in place since 1928. The old rail was replaced with 115-pound welded rail.

After unusually heavy rains, a huge beaver dam burst near Sharon, Vermont, early on the morning of August 7, 1990, releasing flood waters that severely weakened the CV roadbed. The unsuspecting crew of northbound Train 447 struck the washout area about 1:00 a.m., and five locomotives and eleven freight cars immediately toppled off the tracks. Two cars stayed upright, but the rest of the equipment was scattered about the area in an indiscriminate heap. Two of the freight cars contained grain, while the others were empty. The two crewmen riding in the cab of the lead unit were taken to the Gifford Memorial Hospital in Randolph for treatment of minor injuries. The conductor, who was riding in the caboose at the end of the fifty-six-car train, was not injured.

Hulcher Professional Services was once again brought in from Gettysburg, Pennsylvania, to clean up the site. Regular service was resumed on the evening of the second day following the derailment. The ensuing investigation showed that the beaver dam had been located approximately a half-mile from the track.

General manager Chris Burger held meetings with the employees during the summer at Palmer, White River Junction, and St. Albans, in an attempt to personally respond to their questions and concerns about their jobs and the company and to listen to their suggestions. About 125 employees attended these meetings, and most of those participating felt that they had been positive and that everyone had learned something.

A startling development occurred on August 10, 1990, when the U.S. Circuit Court of Appeals set aside the Interstate Commerce Commission's 1988 order that transferred the Boston & Maine's Conn River Line to Amtrak, which in turn immediately sold it to the CV. In filing the appeal, the B&M essentially claimed that condemnation procedures had not been followed and that the transfer of the line was thus unconstitutional. Amtrak also appealed the ICC decision, claiming that the sale price was too high, while Canadian Pacific Railway officials argued that they had been put at a competitive disadvantage by the order. Despite this decision, operations continued as usual while the various legal departments renewed their activities and the matter went to the U. S. Supreme Court.

Just before daybreak on the morning of January 19, 1988, 100-car Train 444 suffered a derailment at Fonda Junction, about four miles north of St. Albans' Italy Yard. The fiftieth car picked the points of the north passing track switch with these results. The site was only a few hundred yards from busy U.S. Route 7, so the lumber disappeared rather rapidly. (Jim Murphy photo)

Traffic was interrupted for a few days as Hulcher Professional Services was called in to spearhead the cleanup work. CV personnel and equipment augmented the Hulcher crew. Eighteen cars had to be recovered and several hundred feet of track had to be rebuilt before operations could resume. The lack of snow, unusual for northern Vermont at this time of the year, made the work much easier. (Jim Murphy photo)

In October, the high court announced that it would review the decision of the U.S. Circuit Court of Appeals concerning ownership of the Conn River Line. It was not until March 25, 1992, however, that the Supreme Court justices reversed the federal appeals court ruling by a six to three vote. They stated that Amtrak and the Interstate Commerce Commission had acted within their authority and that the need that Amtrak had established for the property must be affirmed.

On September 24, Burlington's City Council adopted an urban renewal plan involving the waterfront. The city appraised the forty-five acres on which it had previously been given an option to

(Left) *Train 444 is passing through the attractive village of Charlestown, New Hampshire, on a wintry February 6, 1988. The next stop to set off and pick up cars will be six miles away at North Walpole, the CV's interchange point with the Green Mountain Railroad. The locomotives on this train are GT 5808, CR 7822, CV 4447, 3614, 4924, and 4445. (Leo Landry photo)*

(Below) *Train 447 has just set off some local cars at White River Junction, and the five locomotives will soon return to their train and head north. Jim Shaughnessy took this photograph from a hillside overlooking the yard on February 9, 1988.*

94   THE CENTRAL VERMONT RAILWAY

This dramatic photograph shows northbound Train 447 blasting through the snow at North Williston, Vermont, on February 17, 1988. This is not an uncommon scene during most Vermont winters. (Alan Irwin photo)

Tom Hildreth photographed northbound Train 447 from the Route 12A overpass at South Charlestown, New Hampshire, on the morning of March 5, 1988. The frozen Connecticut River is much in evidence in the background.

Three GP-9's are taking Train 556, the Burlington wayfreight, out of the CV yard in Burlington after interchanging cars with the Vermont Railway. Just ahead is the brick-lined, curving tunnel under North Avenue. Soon after this photo was taken, the two rear units were sold to the Lamoille Valley Railroad on March 8, 1988. (Nathaniel Cobb photo)

Five recently acquired GP-38AC's are bringing Train 444 into Palmer, Massachusetts, on May 12, 1988. Note that all five units happen to be arranged in consecutive number order—an operational and numerical rarity! (Dan Foley photo, courtesy Alan Irwin)

Canadian National, Grand Trunk, and Central Vermont power is being serviced at St. Albans on June 11, 1988. During certain periods of the day, this was an unusually busy facility. (Jim Shaughnessy photo)

A few carloads of lumber behind two Lamoille Valley locomotives are approaching Newton Road about three miles north of Italy Yard. At this time, the LVRC had trackage rights between Fonda Junction and St. Albans where traffic between the two roads was interchanged. The access road adjacent to the mainline once held the track of the CV's former St. Armand Subdivision. This photograph was taken by Brian Irwin on June 11, 1988.

Train 447 blasts through Richmond, Vermont, at 40 miles per hour on August 2, 1988, on its way to St. Albans. At this time, the large building on the right housed the editorial and business offices of Mark Smith's Locomotive & Railway Preservation *magazine. (Gary Knapp photo)*

In the 1980s, Italy Yard in St. Albans tended to be a very busy place during the morning hours. On September 1, 1988, CV Nos. 5808 and 4559 are picking up a cut of cars on the left that will be added to the Burlington wayfreight. GP-9 No. 4928 and a trailing unit are working as switchers on this day. The CN power on the right has come in on Train 444 and will take Train 447 north later in the day. (Alan Irwin photo)

98   THE CENTRAL VERMONT RAILWAY

George J. Harmon, the CV's late chief mechanical officer, was honored by having a locomotive named in his memory. (His name appears under the number on the cab.) The enginehouse crew poses on the walkways of GP-9 No. 4559 at the dedication ceremony on August 22, 1988. Harmon's brother Bob, also a mechanical department official, stands on the second step. (Jim Murphy photo)

purchase at $1.6 million. The railroad, on the other hand, determined that the land was worth $9.14 million. With such a disparity in values, a third appraiser was brought in to take testimony from each party and to try to reach an agreement. The appraiser was allowed to adjust either figure by 20 percent toward the middle. In other words, the city's figure could be adjusted upward to $1.92 million, while the railroad's appraisal could be adjusted downward to $7.53 million.

When the final figures were tallied at the end of the year, it was learned that the CV had suffered a loss of $1.3 million in 1990. Revenues decreased from the previous year's level, but expenses were also reduced. The number of employees was down 14 percent from 1989, which resulted in a reduction in labor expense of $2.1 million. Some of this decrease, however, was offset by a drastic jump in the price of locomotive fuel. Before the Gulf War, the CV was paying sixty-four cents a gallon, but by the time hostilities ceased, the price was eighty-six cents. According to chief mechanical officer Bob Harmon, the CV was using about 1.8 million gallons of fuel a year. Thus, this price increase cost the CV nearly $400,000.

The number of carloads handled in 1990 was 33,714, down from 34,981 the previous year. The continuing recession in the Northeast, coupled with intense competition from truckers and other railroads, resulted in significant decreases in lumber and newsprint traffic. However, growth did occur in some areas. Contracts covering wheat and steel brought new traffic to the CV. In addition, sixty to seventy cars per week of flyash from the recently built power plant at Montville, Connecticut, moved northward for the entire year to Bellows Falls (North Walpole), where it was interchanged with the Green Mountain Railroad. Passenger revenues also increased as Amtrak operated over the length of the CV for the entire year.

State, local, and federal funds totaling $1.67 million were received in 1990. This money was

Two GP-9's with dramatically different paint schemes have been assigned to a work train on September 25, 1988. We see the train of about 24 hoppers loaded with ballast heading southbound through Westminster, Vermont. (Ken Houghton photo)

Alco RS-11 No. 3612 is headed for Richford, Vermont, and the Richford Branch's interchange with the Canadian Pacific in frigid conditions on January 4, 1989. The eastbound train is skirting the frozen Missisquoi River just west of East Berkshire. The lettering on the locomotive has been cleverly modified to read "LV." Because the CV's bridge at Sheldon Junction had been partially dismantled, for a few months the Lamoille Valley operated trains from Morrisville to Richford and St. Albans over CV and LVRC tracks. (Alan Irwin photo)

Three GP-9's, each in a different paint scheme, are ready to take a southbound train out of the yard at Palmer, Massachusetts. Ken Houghton took this photo on a cloudless March 10, 1989. In a dedication ceremony at St. Albans on August 22, 1988, the lead locomotive was named "George J. Harmon" to honor the road's late chief mechanical officer.

Shortly before noon on Friday, March 31, 1989, the second, third, and fourth cars of Train 447 derailed near Vernon, Vermont. The company tank car containing locomotive fuel is being raised by a huge crane. The scene was cleared in short order, and service was interrupted only briefly. (Leo Landry photo)

THE CENTRAL VERMONT RAILWAY

used to help offset the cost of various capital improvements—primarily crossing and signal upgrading and track improvements at Willimantic, Brattleboro, Cornish (NH), White River Junction, Essex Junction, Burlington, and St. Albans. The CV also acquired a new freight house and unloading ramp in Brattleboro.

Early in February 1991, Amtrak announced its decision to make the CV's entire line via New London the permanent route for the *Montrealer*. As a consequence of this decision, the $1.8 million not previously spent on the Conn River Line's rehabilitation in 1988 was made available for improvements on this route.

Fourteen miles of welded rail was installed between Brattleboro and Westminster, while other upgrading work included twenty thousand new ties, ten thousand tons of stone ballast, and the lengthening of thirty-four highway crossing signal circuits to permit higher train speeds. In addition, the installation of a new radio system greatly improved communications between dispatchers, car control clerks, train crews, and other personnel along the line.

The long battle over the Burlington waterfront reached another milestone on May 17, 1991, when previously agreed-upon independent appraiser Charles Thompson of Concord, New Hampshire, set a value of $1.92 million on forty-five acres of this land. This figure was 20 percent more than the city's $1.6 million figure, but far less than the $9.14 million the CV felt it was worth. According to the final agreement, the city would assume the cost of any necessary environmental cleanup of the property. Meanwhile, in March, Burlington voters approved a bond issue of up to $1 million to purchase this land.

Finally, at 7:00 p.m. on September 6, Burlington mayor Peter Clavelle and CV general manager Chris Burger signed the historic agreement whereby the forty-five waterfront acres became the property of the City of Burlington. Legal considerations dictated that one-half of this land be preserved as public, open space. Much of this land is fill that was brought in by the railroad during the mid-1800s to provide facilities for Burlington's rapidly growing lumber market. Burlington was,

Chop-nosed GP-9 No. 4926 leads five other units and Train 447 through the Connecticut River Valley south of Charlestown on June 1, 1989. (Leo Landry photo)

102 THE CENTRAL VERMONT RAILWAY

Train 444 is kicking up a cloud of dust at the crossing just north of the Montpelier Junction station on a rare Saturday morning run on July 15, 1989. The train order stand and the obsolete 41000 series wooden boxcars add to the scene. (Alan Irwin photo)

Amtrak service has just been restored over the CV after a major track rehabilitation project on the former Boston & Maine line in Southern Vermont was completed. The lead locomotive is flying both American and Canadian flags as the train makes its way across the long East Alburg trestle on July 17, 1989. (Gary Knapp photo)

THE CENTRAL VERMONT RAILWAY 103

The CV experienced a major derailment at Dummerston, Vermont, a few miles north of Brattleboro, on October 20, 1989. Much of the damaged equipment as well as the rebuilt right of way is evident in this photograph taken by Tom Hildreth six days later.

Southbound Train 444 with No. 5804 leading and Train 562 share Palmer Yard on January 3, 1990. A large number of cars moved through the compact Palmer Yard every 24 hours. (Stephen D. Carlson photo)

in fact, the country's third largest lumber port in the 1860–1880 era.

General manager Chris Burger announced on September 12 that nineteen of the railroad's thirty-eight clerical workers and management personnel would be laid off as economic conditions forced the company to continue downsizing. It was originally planned that CV as well as Duluth, Winnipeg & Pacific administrative work would be transferred to Detroit. However, this would have required a modification in the existing labor agreements and the idea was dropped. Some of these positions had, in fact, become redundant as increased use of computers enabled the company to combine some of its administrative and supervisory activities. The projected layoffs were expected to take place over the following sixteen months. The company now had 175 people on the payroll.

During the summer of 1991, track gangs installed more than twenty-four thousand new ties, five sets of switch timbers, and 13.8 miles of 112-pound welded rail in Massachusetts and Connecticut. In addition,

The CV's version of a rotary plow is at work clearing a light snowfall from Italy Yard in St. Albans on February 7, 1990. The building in the background for many years housed the CV's dispatching and car control offices as well as facilities for train crews. (Gary Knapp photo)

This beautiful mid-winter night photograph of CV Train 447 was taken at North Walpole, New Hampshire, on January 22, 1990. No. 5808, the lead unit, was wrecked at Sharon, Vermont, eight months later. It was repaired by Conrail at Altoona, Pennsylvania, and returned to service. (Leo Landry photo)

Train 444 was photographed by Jim Shaughnessy at Oakland, about five miles south of St. Albans, on February 18, 1990. These heavy southbound trains ran six days a week and normally required five or six units of head-end power.

CV 4134, GT 4136, and CV 4928 have pumped up the train line, the brake test has been completed, and these units are ready to take a southbound train out of Palmer on February 18, 1990. (Ken Houghton photo)

Grand Trunk GP-9R No. 4606 poses with Amfleet coaches and an Amtrak F-40 in the Green Mountain Railroad's Island Yard at Bellows Falls in May 1990. This was an Operation Lifesaver special that was awaiting a run over the CV to White River Junction. (Fred G. Bailey photo)

ten thousand tons of ballast were spread and 120 miles of track was surfaced. Nineteen temporary workers were hired to assist with the welded-rail program, which began on September 19 and was completed on schedule on October 24. Amtrak funding of $1.7 million was used for these projects.

An overhead highway bridge on Gentes Road in Essex Junction was replaced with a new concrete structure during the year. The original bridge had been built in 1910 to eliminate a grade crossing, but in recent years it had deteriorated to the point where the load limit on it had been reduced to six thousand pounds. During the demolition of the old bridge and construction of the new one by the R. S. Audley Company, the CV installed a temporary crossing at grade.

Citing increasing competitive pressures from both larger Class I carriers and the trucking industry, as well as a growing demand for point-to-point service at lower rates, the management of Canadian National and Grand Trunk Corporation announced at the end of 1991 that the parent company and its three U.S. affiliates would be united and henceforth known as "CN North America." It was felt that by combining marketing and operations, CN customers would be able to deal with a single commercial entity to obtain "seamless" transportation service across Canada and into the United States.

In 1991, the CV posted a $200,000 net income, an improvement over 1990's $1.3 million loss. The sale of the waterfront property in Burlington netted the company about $1.2 million, which did much to offset the road's $1.5 million loss from operations. Unfortunately, revenues were down 8 percent from the previous year's figure, the result of a decline in carloads handled as well as a decrease in the average revenue per car. Important

Limestone is being loaded into covered hoppers at Milton, Vermont, on June 13, 1990. These cars will soon be picked up by a southbound train for movement to the CV's Southern Division. (George Dutka photo, CV Railway Historical Society collection)

Speno rail-grinding equipment RMS-12, Unit 121, was at work at Putney, Vermont, on June 20, 1990. This equipment grinds the inside edges of worn rails to proper contour. The passenger car is used to house and feed the crew. (Leo Landry photo)

A CV detour train is arriving on Green Mountain trackage at Bellows Falls on July 24, 1990. The 44-car train will soon return to its home rails, which can be seen in the foreground. The author, a GMRC conductor, was waiting for the CV train to clear so his GMRC Train XR-1 could proceed northward to Chester and Rutland. (Leo Landry photo)

Locomotives wrecked in the August 7, 1990, washout near Sharon, Vermont, have been towed to Italy Yard in St. Albans for disposition. The first unit in this photo is No. 5803, so badly damaged that it was scrapped. No. 5804 suffered little damage and was promptly repaired by the GTW at Battle Creek. The other units seen here, Nos. 5809, 5808, and 5807, were severely damaged and were rebuilt by the Conrail Juniata Shops at Altoona, Pennsylvania. (Alan Irwin photo)

THE CENTRAL VERMONT RAILWAY 109

Portions of the Richford Branch were torn up in the fall of 1990. CV No. 3602 is the power on the dismantling train on November 8, 1990. Pausing for fellow employee Jim Murphy's camera at Chadwick Siding, 5.59 miles from St. Albans, are conductor Tim Coleman on the left, brakeman Frank Coleman, and engineer Mike Flanagan.

commodities such as lumber, building materials, wire, copper, and paper were all down in 1991 as the region's economy remained sluggish.

During the year, the 2,600 cars that were interchanged with Conrail at Palmer produced revenue of about $2 million. Labor expenses for the year were down 11 percent, while operating expenses in general showed a decrease of 13 percent from the previous year.

Since January 1, 1992, the nation's locomotive engineers have been required to be certified and to have evidence of that fact in their possession while operating a locomotive. Engineers that had been promoted prior to this date were certified under provisions of a grandfather clause. Recertification, however, is required at least every three years. This process includes vision and hearing testing, operating and safety rules examina-

The Central Vermont Railway Historical Society's first annual convention was hosted by the Central Vermont Railway at St. Albans during the summer of 1991. Many contributors of material to this volume are in this group, including general manager Chris Burger, standing at the end of the turntable, third from the left. Jim Murphy, who took the photo, is standing behind Chris Burger's right shoulder.

With GP-38AC's 5802, 5806, and 6209 providing the power, Train 447 is working its way north through rural North Belchertown, Massachusetts, on a beautiful sunny December 14, 1990. No. 6209 is former Detroit, Toledo & Ironton No. 209. (Stephen D. Carlson photo)

An early winter sun highlights a Southern Division Santa Train at Palmer on December 15, 1990. The venerable GP-9 No. 4559 "George J. Harmon," four coaches, and two cabooses were used to give children, their parents, and other local residents a short train ride. Santa Claus was on board to listen to gift requests and to dispense candy. (Stephen D. Carlson photo)

THE CENTRAL VERMONT RAILWAY 111

Northbound Train 447 is pulling out of the CV's yard at Brattleboro on February 25, 1991. Several of the units on this train are being ferried back to St. Albans after handling heavy southbound trains to the Southern Division. (Tom Hildreth photo)

GP-9's Nos. CV 4926 and GT 4918 provide the power for this northbound train at Palmer on May 12, 1991. The hopper cars were used for hauling flyash from Montville, Connecticut, to Virginia and West Virginia via the CV, Green Mountain Railroad, Vermont Railway, CP/D&H, and CSX. An average of about 60 carloads a week were handled over this routing. (Leo Landry photo)

112 THE CENTRAL VERMONT RAILWAY

Southbound Train 444 passes under a highway overpass at Claremont Junction, New Hampshire, in the early 1990s. The CV interchanges traffic here with short-line Claremont & Concord Railroad. (Scott Whitney photo)

During the summer of 1991, GP-38AC No. 5800 leads a long southbound train out of St. Albans. Virtually all of the loads in this train were received from the Canadian National at Montreal. (Roger Wiberg photo)

THE CENTRAL VERMONT RAILWAY 113

tions, documented field supervision, classroom instruction, and checks of motor vehicle records. In order to become a certified engineer after January 1, 1992, employees had to complete a lengthy and intensive program of supervised on-the-job training combined with classroom work covering all phases of the job.

Early in 1992, the first visible changes related to the formation of CN North America were noted. The CV's marketing activities were integrated into a system-wide program. A three-person New England marketing team was formed, headed by the CV's Don Caster.

CN motive power began running between Montreal and Palmer on Trains 444 and 447. As a result, thirteen of the CV's twenty-one assigned locomotives were released for service elsewhere on the CN North America system. The CV retained eight GP-

(Right) *Southbound Train 324 is crossing the New England Power Company canal at Bellows Falls at ten miles per hour on a snowy day during the winter of 1991–92. This photo was taken from above the north portal of the short railroad tunnel that takes trains under the Bellows Falls village square. (Fred G. Bailey photo)*

Train 444 is working its way up the stiff grade south of St. Albans in the summer of 1991. Roger Wiberg took this photo from the Route 7 overpass about one mile from the south end of Beartown Yard at St. Albans.

The Valley Railroad's Chinese-built 2-8-2 was used in the filming of "Ethan Frome" on the Green Mountain Railroad on January 25, 1992. Here the steam locomotive, piloted by the CV's GP-38AC No. 5801, passes through Stafford Springs, Connecticut, on January 22. (Leo Landry photo)

(Left) *The Valley Railroad's nearly new 2-8-2, with its bell ringing, passes the Palmer yard office on January 22, 1992, en route to the GMRC at Bellows Falls and its "Ethan Frome" film assignment three days later. (Leo Landry photo)*

38 locomotives—six to handle trains between Palmer and New London and two based at St. Albans. The Mechanical Department personnel with lifetime jobs thus had little work to do as the CN units were serviced in Montreal.

During the spring, flood waters and ice severely damaged a 125-year old stone arch culvert at Sharon. Broad Brook, which passes under both the CV right of way and Town Road No. 3, was backed up by huge chunks of ice in the nearby White River. Some of this ice was forced into the culvert, loosening much of the stonework.

Miller Construction Company of Windsor was brought in to drive sheet piling to stabilize the east side of the fill, and CV crews installed temporary supports in the culvert and built a rail guard at the culvert's inlet to prevent additional damage by ice or debris. Track foremen walked trains over the area for two weeks while monitoring the sta-

The date is March 1, 1992, in Middlesex, Vermont, and we are looking at the last Train 444 powered by locomotives maintained at St. Albans. The next Train 444, which ran on March 3, was powered by CN run-through units. Within six weeks, all CV power was returned to the GTW except for eight 5800s that were used on local freights. (Alan Irwin photo)

Amtrak's late-running Montrealer *is fighting the Blizzard of '93 at Charlestown, New Hampshire. When a heavy March snowfall made highways impassable, photographer Fred Bailey had to settle for just one shot of the northbound train this day—from his backyard!*

bility of the fill. The railroad, the Town of Sharon, and the state then worked together to formulate a plan to fund the $600,000 in permanent repairs required to rebuild the damaged structure. This work was completed in the fall.

Soon after the Lamoille Valley Railroad canceled its lease on the Sheldon Junction-Richford segment of the Richford Subdivision, the CV began proceedings to abandon the line. No traffic had moved over the road for more than two years, and a survey of local customers indicated that there was little possibility that business would again return to these rails.

After receiving the Interstate Commerce Commission's approval to abandon the remaining 17.44 miles of trackage on the Richford Subdivision in late March 1992, the crossing signals were taken down and the rails removed. The seven miles of welded rail was then utilized on the main line, while the jointed rail was sold as scrap. Sadly, after providing rail service to the communities of Sheldon, Enosburg, East Berkshire, and Richford for 120 years, the Richford Branch was now gone.

Effective August 3, through freights 444 (southbound) and 447 (northbound) were renumbered 324 and 323 respectively. These changes were made so that the numbers of these trains would coincide with the CN numbering system, which assigns numbers in the 300 series to all through freight trains. Later, on November 29, the numbers of Amtrak's *Montrealers* were changed from 623 and 624 (CV numbers) to 61 and 60. These changes were made so that the *Montrealer* would carry the same Amtrak numbers for the entire length of the run between Montreal and Washington. It should be pointed out that the numbers assigned to these trains are the only exception to the CV's long-standing policy of using even numbers on southbound trains and odd numbers for northbound trains. The reason for this is that the numbers are part of the Amtrak numbering system whereby even numbers are assigned to eastbound trains and odd numbers to westbound trains. In the Amtrak system, the *Montrealer* is considered an eastbound train.

The CV's financial status improved somewhat during 1992. The company earned $19.4 million in revenue, while recording a net income of $847,000. Nonetheless, in March 1993, the CV's 171 employees were informed that parent Cana-

Southbound Train 324 has crested the CV's ruling grade at Roxbury and is passing picturesque Mud Pond on the descending grade in April 1992. (Nathaniel Cobb photo)

Three GP-38AC's have brought Train 562 into Palmer in May 1992 and are now delivering cars from that train to the Conrail interchange. Most of these units were painted in Grand Trunk colors with CV lettering. (Richard C. Barnett photo)

(Left) Canadian National No. 9649 leads a southbound train onto the high bridge over the Sugar River north of Claremont, New Hampshire, in July 1992. (Scott J. Whitney photo)

dian National Railway was again considering selling its 325-mile Central Vermont subsidiary. A task force was appointed to explore the matter, and in late October the CN announced that the CV would indeed be sold to the highest bidder.

In the fall of 1993, CN North America announced that it would solicit bids from qualified operators and that it would also consider a stock-ownership plan (soon to become known by its acronym, ESOP) whereby employees would eventually own the railroad. CV general manager Chris Burger, who was instrumental in the development of the plan, acknowledged that it would result in the loss of about forty jobs. Inherent in ESOP, also, was a reduction in current wage scales and significant modifications in the existing work rules. Valumetrics, Inc. of Oakbrook, Illinois, and the Chicago law firm of Oppenheimer, Wolff, and Donnelly were retained by the Canadian National to work with general manager Burger and the CV's chief financial officer, Michael Duchesneau, to formulate ESOP.

(continued on page 139)

A special train has just brought excursionists from the Boston area to Bellows Falls on February 25, 1989. Amtrak equipment was used on this train, which has stopped in front of the Bellows Falls passenger station. A Green Mountain Railroad Alco RS-1 and pristine 98-year-old ex-Rutland Railroad combine No. 260 pose on GMRC trackage. (Leo Landry photo)

A washout on the Central Vermont resulted in Train 444 being detoured over the Vermont Railway for 67 miles between Burlington and Rutland and then over the Green Mountain Railroad for 52 miles between Rutland and Bellows Falls. This train is passing the venerable Chester depot late on the morning of July 24, 1990, and is about to cross Route 103. About half of the consist was left on the Vermont Railway north of Middlebury after a car near the middle of the train derailed. (Leo Landry photo)

119

This power from Train 562 has just delivered cars to the Conrail interchange track at Palmer, Massachusetts, in November 1990. The freshly painted No. 4559 was one of the CV's last green and yellow GP-9's. (Richard C. Barnett photo)

Steve Carlson took this impressive night photo of Train 555 at Palmer on December 14, 1990. These three GP-9's were about 33 years old when this photo was taken.

120

Rich Barnett photographed Train 555 winding its way through Stafford Springs, Connecticut, in mid-April 1991. The roof of the passenger station shows above the two head cars on the train.

Train 447 has just emerged from the Bellows Falls tunnel and the engineer is sounding the 5808's horn for Depot Street crossing. The four units will set off the two head cars on the Green Mountain Railroad's interchange track at North Walpole, New Hampshire, about one mile ahead. Fred G. Bailey took this photo in August 1991.

Train 444 is crossing the Duxbury Bridge on May 25, 1992. For a short time, the train's early departure from St. Albans made it possible to have the sun directly on the head end of the train when viewed from the north side of the bridge. One span of the bridge bears the barely discernible lettering, "Central Vermont—Green Mountain Route." This slogan was applied to several of the road's girder bridges prior to World War II. (Alan Irwin photo)

The backwaters of the Connecticut River and the hills of New Hampshire provide an idyllic setting for six-unit Train 324 as it heads south out of Brattleboro on October 4, 1992. The rear of the train has not yet cleared the Brattleboro yard. (Stephen D. Carlson photo)

122

Fall colors have started to appear as Train 324, powered by three CN road units, works its way south through East Northfield, Massachusetts, on October 12, 1992. This locale, about ten miles south of Brattleboro, is a junction point with the Springfield Terminal (Guilford's Boston & Maine) Railroad. (Stephen D. Carlson photo)

Steve Carlson took this night photo of northbound Train 323 at Palmer at 12:35 a.m. on January 12, 1993. The light snow cover is misleading—a very harsh winter soon followed.

123

The yard tracks at North Walpole are covered by snow on the night of March 14, 1993, when Leo Landry was on hand to photograph the passing of Amtrak's Montrealer. *The amount of snow on the front of the lead unit shows why this CN locomotive was added to provide extra power on this stormy night.*

Southbound Train 444 works upgrade between Montpelier Junction and Roxbury, Vermont, during the summer of 1993. Nearly 20,000 horsepower are represented by these six locomotives as they battle the road's ruling grade. This scene is typical of that found along much of the CV's route through four New England states. (Chris J. Burger photo)

Northbound Train 555 skirts the Thames River at Smith Cove, Connecticut, in June 1993. The three GP-38's were typical power for this train. (Richard C. Barnett photo)

Northbound Train 323 passes through hayfields near Westminster, Vermont, on a beautiful summer day in June 1993. The power on this train will run through to Montreal. (Fred G. Bailey photo)

After Canadian National units began running south of St. Albans in the early 1990s, finding a CV unit in the lead became a "railfan's dream." In June 1993, Fred Bailey was at Charlestown, New Hampshire, to capture this now rare event as GP-38AC No. 5810 was the leader on Train 323.

The beautifully maintained No. 5810 is on display at White River Junction opposite an old Boston & Maine 4-4-0 during the 1993 "Glory Days of Railroading" activities. The area's long and rich railroad history is highlighted each September by this two-day event. (Chris J. Burger photo)

CV Train 555 is making its way through Willimantic, Connecticut, on October 24, 1993. This train regularly handled a heavy volume of Southern Division traffic. (Stephen D. Carlson photo)

The dam at Eagleville, Connecticut, makes an unusually picturesque setting for Train 555. Steve Carlson took this photo on December 11, 1993.

Bill Gleason provided the lighting and Steve Carlson took this classic night photo of CN-powered Central Vermont Train 324 at Brattleboro on December 26, 1993.

128

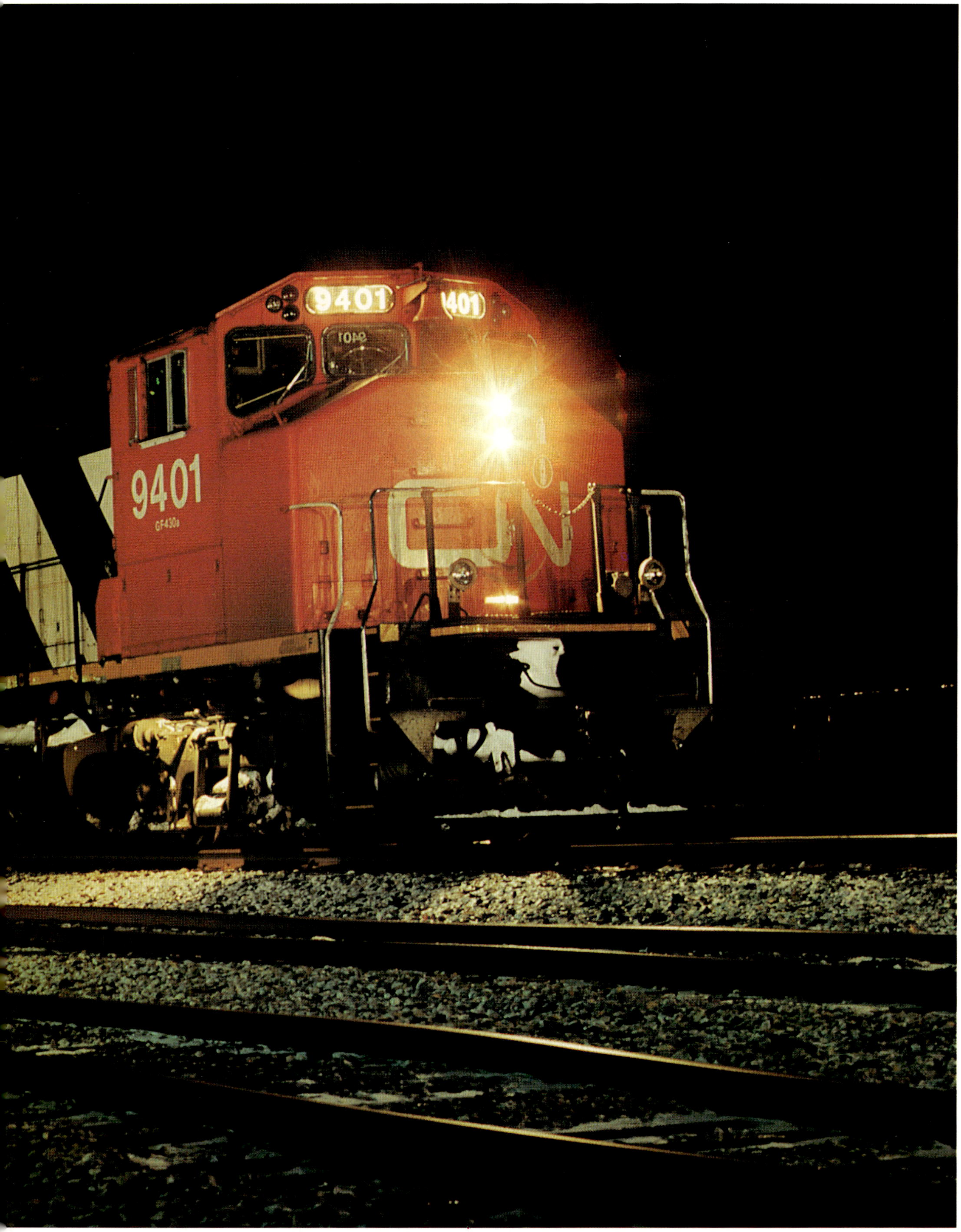
9401
9401
9401
GF430a

Camels Hump provides a beautiful backdrop for Train 324 as it makes its way through Waterbury, Vermont, on a sunny winter day in January 1994. (Roger Wiberg photo)

GP-38AC No. 5810 and the road's Jordan spreader have nearly finished cleaning out St. Albans' Italy Yard in February 1994. The equipment is approaching North Junction on Track 102. (Nathaniel Cobb photo)

The wide Thames River and the lush Connecticut hillside provide a beautiful setting for Train 555 at Norwich in May 1994. (Richard C. Barnett photo)

Southbound Train 324 is meeting Train 323 at Roxbury, Vermont on June 3, 1994. Engineer Mike Flanagan's northbound train is on the siding, and he is about to make a roll-by inspection of the other train. (Jim Shaughnessy photo)

Train 324 hits the CV-GMRC diamond at Bellows Falls on a sunny afternoon in June 1994. GMRC GP-9 No. 1849, trailing the train's road power, was en route to Palmer, Massachusetts, to work for the Massachusetts Central under a short-term lease. (Fred G. Bailey)

Train 324 crosses the bridge at Duxbury, Vermont, on June 3, 1994. The head car contains limestone and was picked up at Milton. It will be delivered to an on-line customer in Connecticut. (Jim Shaughnessy photo)

Southbound Train 444 and the Burlington wayfreight are meeting at Milton on the afternoon of November 17, 1994. The wayfreight has brought 20 cars of woodchips to the Burlington Electric Department's generating plant, and the empties are on the way back to East Swanton for reloading. This was the only CV train still using a caboose at this time. (Gary Knapp photo)

Morning scheduling of Train 323 northward from Brattleboro provided photographers with excellent light for filming this train during the CV's final years. Vermont's snow-capped Mt. Ascutney and the Claremont High Bridge at West Claremont, New Hampshire, as seen from the shore of the Sugar River on the seldom-photographed east side of the bridge, provided this spectacular view of Train 323 on January 29, 1995. (Fred G. Bailey photo)

133

Local freight 562 has just picked up two empty lumber cars from a customer at Belchertown, Massachusetts, near the end of the CV's operations. (Stephen D. Carlson photo)

The last CV Burlington wayfreight, Train 556, is about to leave Italy Yard on February 3, 1995. The head car is an empty that will be set off in Milton, while the large MacIntyre tank cars contain fuel oil that was loaded at Montreal. (Jim Shaughnessy photo)

This unusual view of the harbor at New London, Connecticut, shows northbound Train 555 skirting the water's edge on September 28, 1992. The cabooseless 14-car train on this day featured GP-38AC's Nos. 5809, 5802, and 5800 on the head end. (George Dutka photo, CV Railway Historical Society collection)

Three Canadian National road units provide the power for southbound Train 324 on October 1, 1992. The train is crossing the long Millers Falls, Massachusetts, bridge with Southern Division traffic. (Stephen D. Carlson photo)

Two immaculate GP-38-AC's, Nos. 5806 and 5808, lead Train 555 across the truss bridge at Palmer on October 1, 1992. No. 5808 had been wrecked at Sharon, Vermont, on August 7, 1990, and was later repaired by Conrail at Altoona, Pennsylvania. (Stephen D. Carlson photo)

136   THE CENTRAL VERMONT RAILWAY

Three CN units are bringing Train 324 into Brattleboro Yard on October 7, 1992. The coal hoppers came off the Green Mountain Railroad at Bellows Falls and are bound for Montville, Connecticut, where they will be loaded with flyash for transport to Virginia and West Virginia. (Stephen D. Carlson photo)

The St. Albans-bound Burlington wayfreight is passing behind a small shopping center on Pearl Street in Essex Junction in December 1992. The head-end cars will go to Montreal, while the large hopper cars will go to East Swanton to be reloaded with woodchips. (Roger Wiberg photo)

An Amtrak special operated for the Mass Bay Division of the RRE is arriving in Bellows Falls on CV trackage in February 1993. Green Mountain Railroad GP-9 No. 1851 is waiting on the CV/GMRC connection to assist in making the switching moves necessary to prepare the passenger train for its return to Boston. (Grace J. Bailey photo)

The lead unit of Train 324 bursts from the Bellows Falls tunnel and onto the Mill Street crossing on a wintry February 14, 1993. (Leo Landry photo)

CV Train 324, with CN GP-40-2W No. 9665 up front, highballs through Westminster, Vermont, in March 1993. Fred Bailey used a telephoto lens to take this photograph.

138 THE CENTRAL VERMONT RAILWAY

A closed meeting was held at St. Albans on October 29 to brief employees on the proposed Employee Stock Ownership Plan. Although no purchase price was disclosed at this time, it was explained that the plan would require obtaining a bank loan for the full amount of the purchase price. Employees would not be asked to make any cash investments, and, as the loan was repaid, they would be credited with stock in direct proportion to their salaries.

At the meeting, Burger and Grand Trunk Corporation vice president R. A. Walker explained that the ESOP would make the road's employees owners and that ESOPs were, in fact, pension plans that are given substantial tax advantages by the government in order to promote employee ownership and profit sharing. Sale of the railroad was inevitable, Burger felt, and he predicted that the job losses and wage reductions proposed by the ESOP would quite likely prove to be less than those required by any other buyer.

Burger's experience on the employee-owned Chicago & North Western had convinced him that the ESOP would provide the greatest benefits to the CV's employees. R. A. Walker told the employees that Grand Trunk Corporation planned a sale under Section 10901 of the ICC regulations, which meant that employees adversely affected would receive no severance pay or labor protection.

CV employees, union officials, and Vermont's politicians all understood that the railroad needed to reduce labor costs in order to stay in business. However, the announcement that laid-off workers would receive no severance pay sparked immediate opposition to the plan.

Most union officials and employees vehemently opposed ESOP from the beginning. They cited the loss of forty jobs, announced pay cuts of 15 to 20 percent, new work rules, and loss of job protection as the primary reasons for opposing the plan. Because the CV would be acquired by a non-railroad entity, Interstate Commerce Com-

Train 324 is leaving White River Junction in the late spring of 1993. Just ahead of the train is a switch known as "Bank," which leads to the B&M/CV interchange tracks. Cars on the head end of this train will be set off in the B&M yard and will be added to those seen at the right. (Grace J. Bailey photo)

Snow is still on the ground in April 1993 as two CN road units and Conrail Leasing GP-38-2 No. 790 pull southbound Train 324 through the yard at Brattleboro. (Richard C. Barnett photo)

mission rules allow non-railroad companies to take over railroads without the imposition of labor protection costs.

The opposition to ESOP was so strong that Vermont's Congressional delegation soon became involved. After meeting on December 1 with about forty unionized employees, Representative Bernard Sanders termed the potential loss of forty jobs to be "unacceptable," and he urged CN and CV officials to negotiate a "mutually satisfactory" sale agreement. Sanders indicated that he was working on legislation that would provide labor protection for the workers. For their part, U.S. Senators Patrick Leahy and James Jeffords requested the Interstate Commerce Commission to hold a public meeting in St. Albans to discuss the pending sale. The ICC denied the request on the grounds that it was "premature."

Meanwhile, in 1993 the CV posted an operating profit for the first time in several years. That is, the company made a profit from its rail operations, exclusive of revenue from sources such as leases and asset sales. Also, for the first time in its history, the CV paid profit-sharing money to its employees (approximately 4 percent of each employee's earnings) except to those represented by the United Transportation Union (UTU), who had not entered into a profit-sharing agreement in the 1980s.

Late in 1993, Canadian National North America (CNNA) began routing intermodal traffic over the CV to the Mass Central Railroad at Palmer, a positive conclusion to the CV's prolonged efforts to obtain such traffic. The Mass Central and CNNA agreement stipulated that the former would serve as CNNA's intermodal facility in the area. Cars were blocked on Train 324 so they could be quickly set out on the Mass Central interchange track at Palmer upon arrival. This traffic increased throughout 1994, amounting to well over 1,500 units. Most of this business was paper from Quebec, although significant traffic also came from Chicago and Toronto.

February 4, 1994, was the deadline for interested parties to submit their initial bids to purchase the CV. By early January, the Massachusetts Central and the Providence & Worcester railroads had made their interest known. The total amount

The Richford Branch was torn up between Sheldon Junction and Richford during the spring and early summer of 1993. The work train that handled the job is backing over Lamoille Valley Railroad trackage at the Route 78 crossing in East Highgate on its way to Sheldon Junction on May 1, 1993. LVRC trackage was needed for this movement because the CV's bridge at Sheldon Junction had been destroyed in a June 1984 derailment. Conductor Wayne Quilliam and track supervisor Gene Trombley are on the end of the car. (Jim Murphy photo)

The scrapping train is backing off the Lamoille Valley main at Sheldon Junction and onto the CV's Richford Branch on May 1, 1993. Within weeks the last rails of the once-busy 115-year-old line will be lifted. (Jim Murphy photo)

To avoid blocking public crossings in Windsor, Vermont, the crew of Train 323 has left most of their train on the long bridge over the Connecticut River and is moving into town with loads of woodpulp that will be set off on the siding of a busy warehousing facility. (Grace J. Bailey photo)

CN run-through power has Train 323 rolling northward under the Route 12A overpass and alongside Route 12 in South Charlestown, New Hampshire, in June 1993. (Fred G. Bailey photo)

Train 324 is crossing the Connecticut River from Windsor, Vermont, to Cornish, New Hampshire. A great blue heron is flying just above the bushes in the right center foreground. Tom Hildreth notes that seconds after he took this October 11, 1993, photograph, the heron did a "zoom climb." The highway covered bridge in the background is reputed to be the longest such structure in the northeast.

of the latter's bid was approximately $30 million, which was comprised of $20,762,000 of P&W common stock and up to $9 million to cover labor protection provisions. This particular offer was well received by many of the CV employees. Initial bids were also received from RailTex, CSF Acquisition Group, and Oakes Development.

On February 18, officials of the CV's parent organization announced that the proposals of four bidders had been selected for further consideration. In addition to the CV management-led Employee Stock Ownership Plan, those still in the running included Oakes Development of St. Louis Park, Minnesota, CSF Acquisition Group based in Morrisville, Vermont; and RailTex, a railroad holding company with headquarters in San Antonio, Texas, owners and operators of twenty-three short lines in the U.S., Canada, and Mexico.

CSF (the initials of owners Clyde and Saundra Forbes, Jr.) operates the New Hampshire & Vermont and the Twin State railroads in New Hampshire, the Lamoille Valley and the Washington County railroads in Vermont, as well as the Florida West Coast Railroad. The deadline for final bids to be submitted was set for April 8, 1994.

Grand Trunk Corporation and Canadian National officials analyzed the offers submitted by the four finalists, and at the May 10 CN directors' meeting the RailTex proposal to purchase the CV for $40 million was accepted. The announcement of this decision to sell the CV to RailTex was not well received by CV employees and their supporters. The workers, their families, and concerned local, state, and federal politicians vowed to fight the sale. At the heart of their discontent was a federal law that exempts non-railroad companies

THE CENTRAL VERMONT RAILWAY   143

Canadian National GP-40-2W No. 9677 is the lead unit on Train 323 as it works the grade near Roxbury in August 1993. This was the first time a CN North America unit was the leading unit on a CV train. (Fred G. Bailey photo)

Train 562, powered by three ex-Grand Trunk Western GP-38AC's, poses for the photographer in Palmer on October 22, 1993. (Stephen D. Carlson photo)

An unusually short southbound Burlington wayfreight is on the passing track at Milton, Vermont, on a sunny late fall day in 1993. The two tank cars are empties that last contained limestone slurry and are being returned to Florence, Vermont, on the Vermont Railway, for reloading. (Nathaniel Cobb photo)

The snow is flying as CN No. 9636 and two sisters lead a train around a sharp curve on the Roxbury Subdivision near Colchester during the winter of 1993–94. (Roger Wiberg photo)

THE CENTRAL VERMONT RAILWAY 145

Train 444 is climbing the grade at Roxbury on December 30, 1993. CN power had been the norm on this train since March 3, 1992. This photo was taken from the Rabbit Hollow Bridge, about a mile north of the top of the long grade. (Alan Irwin photo)

(Right) *The CV's last general manager, Chris Burger (on the left), and his Green Mountain Railroad counterpart, Jerry Hebda, strike a railfan's pose outside the GMRC office building in Bellows Falls in January 1994. (Fred G. Bailey photo)*

from labor protection costs in acquiring railroads. As a railroad holding company, RailTex is not legally considered to be a railroad company.

Within days, unionized employees organized a statewide rally to be held in St. Albans on June 11. Labor attorney Ed Garvey of Labor Strategies, Inc. of Madison, Wisconsin, was retained to assist the workers in planning and conducting their opposition to the pending sale of the CV to RailTex. In addition, the workers organized the Workers United for Justice on the Central Vermont Railroad to help carry on their fight.

RailTex president and chief executive officer Bruce Flohr announced in late May that his company planned to offer jobs to seventy-eight CV employees and that those not hired would be offered work on a first-hire basis on any of RailTex's twenty-one other roads in the U.S. Railtex would,

146   THE CENTRAL VERMONT RAILWAY

Flohr said, pay the workers' relocation expenses and provide medical benefits while they awaited jobs on the other railroads. He also noted that wages for those hired would be approximately 15 percent less than the CV's pay scales.

Meanwhile, Vermont's congressional delegation was taking steps to block the sale—or at least provide job protection if the sale was approved. Representative Bernard Sanders was particularly active as he introduced a bill in the House (H.R. 3866) that would require the Interstate Commerce Commission to provide labor protection as a condition of approval for any rail line transfers.

Senators Patrick Leahy and James Jeffords wrote letters to the ICC asking that CV employees be granted job protection, and soon thereafter they were co-sponsors of a Senate bill that would grant labor protection to displaced workers. This had become the key issue because in the mid-1980s the unionized workers had negotiated job security and attractive severance benefits in return for years of frozen wages. Now the workers and their families felt betrayed because of this provision in the law.

On July 7, the Labor and Human Resources subcommittee on labor, of which Senator Jeffords was a member, held a hearing at St. Mary's Parish Hall in St. Albans to take testimony regarding the pending sale of the CV to RailTex. Representative Bernard Sanders, an ICC official, CV labor representatives, as well as CV and RailTex officials testified during the two-and-one-half hour hearing.

Hearings and opposition notwithstanding, the Grand Trunk Corporation issued a "Notice of Clos-

The southbound Montrealer *makes its brief scheduled stop at Essex Junction on a cold evening in early January 1994. From the snowflakes dancing in the headlight beam, it is apparent that a light snowfall is descending on the area. (Alan Irwin photo)*

The Jordan spreader is clearing tracks in Italy Yard during the harsh 1993–94 winter. When general manager Chris Burger arrived in the fall of 1989, he was informed that the spreader was inoperative and hadn't been used for at least twelve years. Burger immediately instructed the mechanical department to get the equipment ready for possible future use, and it was pressed into service several times in the ensuing years. (Chris J. Burger photo)

Three Canadian National road units are rolling Train 324 through Colchester in January 1994. Mile post 112 indicates that the train has traveled 19 miles from the south yard limit board at St. Albans (CP 131) and that it will leave the Roxbury Subdivision for the Palmer Sub at Windsor in another 112 miles. (Roger Wiberg photo)

148   THE CENTRAL VERMONT RAILWAY

GP-38AC No. 5810 and caboose 4044 are on display on the Burlington waterfront during the city's annual Winter Festival. A large crowd filed through the locomotive cab and the caboose on this very cold but sunny day in February 1994. This was the CV's second appearance at this event, and the equipment was a popular attraction for old and young alike. (Chris J. Burger photo)

Northbound Train 555 passes through Belchertown, Massachusetts, in March 1994 with a train consisting primarily of empties being returned to the Canadian National. Six-axle CN power such as No. 5034 had started running here only a short time before Rich Barnett shot this wintry scene.

THE CENTRAL VERMONT RAILWAY 149

ing" statement to the CV's union and management officials in late July in compliance with federal law. This document stated the parent company's intent to sell its assets and cease doing business on or about October 1, 1994. The law requires a notice of at least sixty days prior to such an event.

In an effort to obtain union and public support, Railtex ran numerous public relations ads in several daily newspapers between late July and early October. These pieces featured such things as RailTex's "can-do" attitude, how the company starts a new railroad with its "GO Team," industry-wide recognition received by some of its roads, RailTex's "value-added service," the company's health care benefits, and one entitled "What If The CV Sale Is Blocked?" A Wednesday, August 10, 1994, *Burlington Free Press* editorial referred to the ads as a "barrage of half-truths."

In a letter to St. Albans mayor Peter DesLauriers in early October, RailTex president Bruce Flohr noted that his company would rename the CV the "New England Central." Flohr stated that he felt the new name "is more representative of the entire region the railroad serves." The RailTex president also announced that thirty-five-year-old Jim Davis, a career railroader who had been with the company since 1990, had been appointed general manager of the New England Central.

Another issue arose over the pending sale when RailTex indicated it wanted most of the documents filed with the Interstate Commerce Commission to be kept secret. The ICC quickly ruled that because of their proprietary nature, items designated as "confidential" or "highly confidential" did not have to be made public.

In response to a request from Vermont's congressional delegation, the ICC held a public hearing in St. Albans on October 19. Because of the large number of people interested in attending, one three-hour session was held in the morning and a second one in the afternoon. Senators Leahy and Jeffords and Representative Sanders all testified, as did labor attorney Ed Garvey and many members of the general public. The CV had videotapes made of the proceedings and also released

A Buyers' Special skirts the Winooski River on March 10, 1994. This immaculate GP-38AC was nearly always used on the CV's public relations trips and demonstrations after it arrived on the property in 1988. (Gary Knapp photo)

as many workers as possible to participate. These sessions were followed by three more days of hearings at the ICC building in Washington.

Meanwhile, the New England Central Railroad Company, Inc., filed its Notice of Exemption with the ICC on October 7. This document fulfilled a legal requirement, officially informing the ICC that New England Central sought approval to purchase the CV. The document also stated that New England Central planned to employ a total of ninety-five workers. The additional seventeen employees over the figure that had been previously announced was due to New England Central's decision to perform additional administrative and locomotive-repair work at St. Albans.

(Right) *CV Train 447 is approaching a point known as the "The Ledges," about one-half mile south of the North Williston Road crossing. Alan Irwin was on the scene on March 12, 1994, about thirty-six hours after freezing rain had fallen on the area.*

(Below) *CN North America SD-40R No. 6005 leads Train 324 southward at South Charlestown, New Hampshire, in May 1994. The dwelling at the left was advertised in railfan publications as a fine home from which to watch trains. When there were no takers, the building was torn down in December 1994. (Fred G. Bailey photo)*

THE CENTRAL VERMONT RAILWAY 151

Vermont's Act 250, one of the nation's toughest land-use control laws, became a public issue in late October when it became known that the agreement to sell the CV to New England Central contained a clause that allows the buyer to circumvent this law. Essentially, the agreement gives the buyer an easement on the land, but ownership of the track and selected equipment. The document, however, provides for the Central Vermont to transfer title of the land at any time in the next forty-nine years at no additional cost. In addition, the agreement calls for the CV to spend up to $100,000 over the next five years to lobby the state legislature to change the law so that railroads will be exempt from its provisions.

The ICC had originally announced that it planned to release its decision on the pending sale of the CV before the end of October. However, on October 27 the commissioners indicated that they would delay the decision until December 10. They felt the extra time was needed to deliberate further on the concerns raised by labor and others at the various hearings held both in Vermont and in Washington. The opponents of the plan viewed the delay as a hopeful sign.

On Friday, December 9, however, the ICC rendered its decision—the sale of the Central Vermont Railway to the RailTex subsidiary was approved! Those opposed to the sale were angered by the decision, and they immediately scheduled a meeting for December 12 to discuss plans for an appeal.

The ICC's decision explicitly exempted RailTex from Section 10901 labor provisions, thus agreeing with RailTex officials that their company is not a rail carrier. The ICC decision, however, did contain a modicum of labor protection for the employees that was based on RailTex's job continuation plan. Specifically, displaced workers would have to be remunerated at half pay for eighteen months, would receive fully funded health insurance coverage for the same period of time, and would receive preferential hiring by other RailTex roads. In addition, CV employees had the option of taking a severance buyout from CN

Old Glory waves a salute to a Canadian National P-40-2W as Train 324 passes the Flock Fibers, Inc. (FFI) plant at North Walpole, New Hampshire, on a summer afternoon in 1994. (Grace J. Bailey photo)

This "accident" is actually an Operation Lifesaver demonstration that was enacted on the Burlington waterfront during the summer of 1994. This photograph by Roger Wiberg graphically illustrates what can happen when a vehicle tries to beat a train at a crossing. As the Operation Lifesaver slogan says, "If it's a tie, you lose."

(Right) *The Burlington wayfreight has just passed the Burlington Electric Department's generating plant located on the Intervale at Burlington in the summer of 1994. The train is approaching the tunnel under North Avenue and will continue on to the Vermont Railway's yard, where these cars will be turned over to the VTR. Northbound cars will also be picked up from the VTR. (Nathaniel Cobb photo)*

North America—the amount to range between $20,000 and $55,000, depending upon years of service and rate of pay.

At the December 12 meeting, the unionized employees overwhelmingly voted to appeal the ICC's decision. In addition to the employees, U.S. Representative Bernard Sanders, aides to senators Patrick Leahy and James Jeffords, state attorney Jeffrey Amestoy, and labor lawyer Ed Garvey were present. Garvey announced at the evening meeting that the unions had petitioned the ICC to delay the sale until their appeal had been heard. However, on December 22 the federal regulators denied the stay request.

Meanwhile, CV general manager Chris Burger resigned his position effective November 30, 1994,

An unusually short Burlington wayfreight makes its way across the Georgia High Bridge on its way back to St. Albans. The long tank car carrying "Dangerous" placards has been placed in this four-car train according to Federal Railroad Administration requirements. (Gary Knapp photo)

In 1993, CV officials requested funding from the State of Vermont to subsidize the cost of applying fire retardant to the East Alburg trestle. The request met with considerable opposition and controversy, primarily because of the pending sale of the railroad. The funding was eventually approved, however, and here we see Bridge & Building foreman Ernie Cheney and his gang beginning the application in September 1994. (Chris J. Burger photo)

The presence of only two units on the head end of Train 323 indicates that the northbound train is a relatively short one. The train is approaching the south switch of the long passing siding at Oakland on a bright fall day in 1994, with only about six miles left to cover on its 182-mile journey from Brattleboro. (Roger Wiberg photo)

New and old passenger equipment rubbed shoulders at White River Junction during the community's "Glory Days of Railroading" celebration held in September 1994. Brand new Amtrak Superliner coaches, built by Bombardier in Barre, Vermont, contrast sharply with the Green Mountain Railroad's ex-Rutland Railroad combine No. 260 that was built 103 years earlier. (Fred G. Bailey photo)

THE CENTRAL VERMONT RAILWAY 159

CV was designated a corporate member of the museum in July 1994. This entitled the railroad to one hundred free one-day passes, which were distributed to employees on a first-come, first-serve basis.

More bad news arrived in CV country on December 14 when Amtrak announced that the well-patronized *Montrealer* would be discontinued effective April 1, 1995. This action was necessary, Amtrak directors determined, because of operating losses incurred by the *Montrealer* ($4.8 million a year, according to Amtrak), a $200 million Amtrak deficit nationally, and proposed reductions in federal funding. In addition to cutting the *Montrealer*, Amtrak officials also announced the elimination of other trains as well as numerous reductions in the frequency of service over much of its national network.

The loss of this important alternative to air and highway travel would result in the abolishment of eight Amtrak ticket agents' and caretakers' jobs, as well as the loss of approximately $1 million in revenue annually that had been earned by the CV and was anticipated by the New England Central. Vermont Governor Howard Dean and the state's congressional delegation immediately asked Amtrak President Thomas Downs to reconsider the decision to eliminate Vermont's only passenger service.

Senators Leahy and Jeffords and Representative Sanders met with Amtrak officials in Washington on January 10 to urge the retention of passenger service in Vermont. In addition to discussing the overnight Montreal-Washington train, other options were also suggested. These included making the *Montrealer* a day train, terminating it at St.

Early on a January 1995 morning, Alan Irwin was on hand to photograph a northbound Amtrak Montrealer *from a cornfield just north of Richmond, Vermont. The well-patronized train is kicking up plenty of fresh snow as it passes cloud-tinged Camels Hump.*

The CV's good housekeeping and maintenance efforts are much in evidence in this photo of No. 5810 on the turntable at the St. Albans enginehouse. (Chris J. Burger photo)

The last CV Train 556 is about to leave St. Albans for Burlington on February 3, 1995. The head car will be set off at Milton, while the rest of the train will be interchanged with the Vermont Railway in Burlington. (Alan Irwin photo)

THE CENTRAL VERMONT RAILWAY   163

Northbound Train 323 has taken the siding at Montpelier Junction on February 3, 1995, to meet Train 324 on the last day of CV operations. The clear, cold day brought out a large number of railfans and photographers to witness and record the day's activities. (Joe Dufresne, Jr., photo)

Immaculate GP-38AC No. 5810 is backing into the Agway plant at St. Albans to spot three loads of feed on February 3, 1995. (Joe Dufresne, Jr., photo)

166   THE CENTRAL VERMONT RAILWAY

The last CV Train 324 crosses the Winooski River at Duxbury in this typical Vermont winter scene. This was the final day that Canadian National power operated south of St. Albans on this train. (Joe Dufresne, Jr., photo)

the train was operated southward by New England Central GO Team personnel, with CV's J. J. Rivers serving as pilot. The consist included twenty-three loads, three empties, and 2,655 tons. This crew returned to Brattleboro early the next morning, Saturday, February 4, with Train 323, thus making it the last CV train to operate.

Later, on Tuesday, February 7, this train ran from Brattleboro to St. Albans, powered by three CN and three CV units that were being returned to the parent company. New England Central had planned to run its first southbound train, 324, on Saturday, February 4, but an eighteen-inch snowstorm, coupled with strong winds, a -20 degree temperature, and a -60 degree wind chill factor resulted in the first southbound run being postponed until Tuesday, February 7.

Train 323, meanwhile, had departed Palmer Thursday evening with W. A. Roberge as conductor and P. A. Celetano at the throttle. CN engines 9581, 9625, and 9505 were trailed by five New England Central units (9531, 9549, 9530, 9521, and 9536). At Brattleboro, the train was taken over by conductor D. W. Boardman and engineer M. J. Flanagan. They arrived in St. Albans at 3:05 p.m. with three loads, fifty-six empties, 2,700 tons. This train was then taken from St. Albans to Montreal by a CN crew using the same power, but with thirteen loads, fifty-seven empties, and 2,934 tons. It was the last CV train to depart St. Albans, Vermont's Rail City.

The Burlington wayfreight, Train 556, left St. Albans at 1:15 p.m. on February 3 with nine loads, four empties, 1,370 tons, behind GP-38 5810. R. P. Livingston was engineer, while co-conductors W. J. Quilliam and M. A. Rivers were in charge of the train. They arrived in Burlington at 2:45 p.m. and departed at 4:30 p.m. with three loads and six empties, 510 tons. This train, the CV's last Burlington wayfreight, arrived in St. Albans at 5:45 p.m..

South of Palmer, Train 562 did local work with engine 5801. D. J. Canon was conductor and L. J.

THE CENTRAL VERMONT RAILWAY 167

Jim Shaughnessy was among the numerous photographers on the scene at St. Albans on February 3, 1995, to record the last departure of CV Train 324. The CV's 130-year-old general office building became the headquarters of the New England Central the following day.

On the last day of operations, CV Train 323 arrived in St. Albans with three CN units and five New England Central GP-38AC's. The latter went into service the following day. These units have just been cut off the train at the north end of the freight yard and are backing into the locomotive service area adjacent to the enginehouse. (Jim Shaughnessy photo)

Szabo was engineer. In addition, Train 555 left New London at 7:30 a.m. behind engines 5806 and 5802 with no loads and fourteen empties, tonnage 452. L. D. Runyon was conductor, and D. J. Daley was engineer. They arrived in Palmer at 1:10 p.m. with seven loads and twenty-eight empties. Meanwhile, N. J. McMahon and N. J. Poulin ran southbound local freight Train 554 with engines 5800 and 5809, handling one load, eight empties, and 350 tons. In addition, the northbound and southbound *Montrealers* operated as usual.

The first New England Central train started work at Palmer on Saturday, February 4 at 8:45 a.m.. The crew pulled the Conrail interchange and went south to become the first Train 554, New London Turn. They returned to Palmer later that day, and the following day this crew took the locomotives to Brattleboro where they went to St. Albans on the first NEC Train 323 on February 7.

In the final analysis, several factors brought the Central Vermont's 150-year history to an end. The loss of much of the local business, particularly on the Northern Division, was a big factor. Traffic had declined over the years to the point where one six-day-a-week through freight in each direction could handle the tonnage as well as much of the local switching. Deregulation allowed rail carriers and trucking companies to set their own freight rates. While the intent of this legislation was sound, it did result in greatly increased competition that the CV seemingly could not meet.

As a result of declining business, losses occurred, employee layoffs became the norm, and morale understandably declined. Unrealistic work rules that mandated inefficiencies in the assignment of personnel and equipment must also be recognized as a major factor in the CV's demise. Times changed, and the CV was no longer a vibrant, busy railroad. Only a small fraction of its capacity and potential was being utilized. The size of the road as well as the volume and nature of its traffic virtually demanded that it be operated as a short line rather than a regional railroad.

For years, many steps were taken by officials of both the CV and its parent company to convert red numbers to black ones on the company's in-

New England Central, RailTex's twenty-fifth North American railroad, commenced operations on February 4, 1995. People on the scene long before that date planning the transition were Mike Brigham (standing) from the corporate headquarters, and NECR general manager Jim Davis. (Jim Murphy photo)

come statements. Unfortunately, this could not consistently and realistically be done. When the parent CN, its own future in jeopardy, could no longer help the CV, the sale of the money-losing subsidiary was inevitable.

For the many CV employees who were offered jobs by successor New England Central and who elected to go with the new company, it will definitely be the beginning of a new era. New employers have new and different ways of doing things. Hopefully, that will work to the advantage of everyone—employees, shippers, and stockholders alike. There should also be some solace in the fact that the CV was sold, not abandoned. The railroad will continue to be operated with many of the same people doing their jobs even better and more efficiently than before.

The New England Central will never be the Central Vermont; nor can the Central Vermont become the New England Central. Yet, in the long run there may be many more similarities than differences between the two companies.

Long live the Central Vermont! May the New England Central successfully serve the region for the next 150 years!

Sources

Ambassador, Quarterly Publication of the Central Vermont Railway Historical Society. All issues—Spring 1990 to Summer 1995 (Volume I No. 1–Volume VI No. 2).

Ambassador, Employees' newsmagazine. Summer 1990–Summer 1992. All 8 issues.

Annual Reports, Central Vermont Railway, 1980–1994.

Burlington Free Press, several issues 1981–1995.

Charlie Vermont, Employees' newsletter. Volume I (2/85)–Volume VI (Spring 1990). All 29 issues.

Personal Interviews:
- Burger, Chris J. — CV manager, 1989–1994
- Irwin, Alan E., M.D. — President, CVRR Historical Society
- Larner, Paul K. — CV trainmaster and rules examiner
- Murphy, Jim — CV dispatcher

St. Albans Messenger, several issues 1981–1995.

About the Author

Author Robert C. Jones has worked on the Canadian Pacific Railway, the Vermont Railway, and the Green Mountain Railroad during his forty-year railroad career. He has performed the duties of sectionman, brakeman, engineer, conductor, and dispatcher, among other jobs, along the way. He is currently employed in train service by the New England Central Railroad.

But railroading is only one of Bob Jones's vocations. He recently retired after teaching high school for thirty-three years, and he is also the author of an impressive library of books and articles on New England railroading. He has written several popular books about Maine's two-foot gauge railroads, including the classic *Two Feet Between the Rails.* Turning his attention to Vermont subjects, he authored the seven volumes of *The Central Vermont: A Yankee Tradition* and co-authored *Vermont's Granite Railroads.* His *Railroads of Vermont, Volumes I, II,* and *Pictorial,* met with widespread acclaim as the definitive work about Vermont's railroads, large and small.

CENTRAL VERMONT RAILWAY DIESEL ROSTER 1980–1995
Prepared by Alan Irwin May 1995

TYPE	NUMBER	DATE BUILT	BUILDER'S NUMBER	NOTES
Alco S-4	8081	9/55	81401	Sold to K&L Feeds, Yantic, CT #1 12/4/87
SW-1200	1509	4/57	22827	Ellis & Eastern #7 (SD) as of 5/2/89
	1510	4/57	22828	To Rinker Materials from GTW 5/2/89
	1511	3/60	25743	Arkansas Eastman 511 as of 2/11/89
RS-11	3600	8/56	81934	To Genesee Valley Leasing 6/16/88
	3601	8/56	81935	To LVRC for parts 3/8/88
	3602(1)	8/56	81936	Scrapped 11/87 Swanton
	3603	8/56	81937	To GV Leasing for parts 10/89
	3604	9/56	81938	To GV Leasing 6/16/88
	3605	9/56	81939	To Winchester and Western 10/7/88 Former DWP Bicentennial unit
	3606	9/56	81940	To Quaboag Transfer 11/85 To Winchester and Western 10/7/88 To Wimpey Minerals 360, Annville, PA Wrecked 1994
	3607	9/56	81941	Arrived from DWP unserviceable 4/12/83 Scrapped Italy Yard 6/18/85
	3608	9/56	81942	To LVRC 3/8/88 Stored U/S
	3609(1)	9/56	82026	Returned 12/79 Cut up 4/81
	3609(2)	11/58	82958	Ex-N&W 367 To W&W 10/7/88. Now Maine Coast 367
	3610	9/56	82027	Arrived from DWP unserviceable 4/12/83 Scrapped Italy Yard 6/18/85
	3611	9/56	82028	To Quaboag Transfer 10/85 To W&W 10/7/88 Scrapped?
	3612	9/56	82029	To LVRC 3/8/88 Sold to Petromont, Montreal, Canada 2/95
	3613	9/56	82030	Scrapped Swanton 11/87
	3614(1)	9/56	82031	Scrapped St. Albans 8/86
GP-18	3602(2)	10/61	26934	Ex-Rock Island 1345 To GTW 9/3/91
	3614(2)	1/60	25451	Ex-Rock Island 1334, To GTW 9/3/91 Both to Georgia Central 3/17/92
Freight GP-9 Phase III	4134	11/58	24964	All 6 currently in service on GTW
	4135	11/58	24965	
	4136	11/58	24966	
	4137	11/58	24967	
	4138	11/58	24968	
	4139	4/59	25433	GTW 4541, Wrecked 1/59 Rebuilt By EMD as 4139
Freight GP-9 Phase II	4441	8/54	19679	Ex-GTW 1765 To SLR 1760 Now 60
	4442	5/56	21449	To SLR 1766
	4445	5/56	21452	To SLR 1768 Now 68

TYPE	NUMBER	DATE BUILT	BUILDER'S NUMBER	NOTES
Freight GP-9 Phase II *(continued)*	4447	6/56	21454	Now SLR 1762
	4448	6/56	21455	To SLR 1758(1) Scrapped 9/94
	4449	6/56	21456	To GTW GPR9 #4604 10/3/89
	4450	6/56	21457	Now SLR 1764
	4542	3/57	22850	Orig. GTW Painted CV by mistake? Kansas Southwestern as of 4/5/91
	4548	3/57	22837	To Huron & Eastern 105 11/90—11/93 Now Delaware Valley 105
	4549	3/57	22838	To GTW 4623 Last unaltered original CV GP-9 when it left St. Albans 9/6/90
	4550	3/57	22839	To GTW 4607 12/14/89
	4551	3/57	22840	To GTW 4605 8/9/89
	4557	3/57	22846	GTW 1/65 to 2/89 Returned 3/29/90 Kansas Southwestern as of 4/5/91
	4558	3/57	22834	Wrecked Sharon, VT 12/89 To GTW GPR9 4613 using a secondhand SP GP-9 hood 9/14/90
	4559	3/57	33835	Dedicated as "George J. Harmon" 8/22/88 Left CV 3/4/92 To Archer-Daniels-Midland, Clinton, IA 9/24/93
Torpedo GP-9 Phase II	4912	1/57	22860	Orig. GTW Kansas Southwestern 4/5/91
	4917	1/57	22865	Orig. GTW In Service on GTW
	4918	1/57	22866	Orig. GTW In Service on GTW
	4919	1/57	22867	Orig. GTW In Service on GTW
	4920	1/57	22868	Orig. GTW In Service on GTW
	4921	1/57	22869	Orig. GTW To GTW GPR9 4622 9/13/21
	4922	1/57	22870	Orig. GTW To GTW GPR9 4628 2/28/92
	4923	3/57	22829	Orig. CVR To GTW GPR9 4612 6/27/90
	4924	3/57	22830	Orig. CVR To GTW GPR9 4617 12/28/90
	4925	3/57	22831	Orig. CVR To GTW GPR9 4609, 3/30/90
	4926	3/57	22832	Orig. CVR To GTW 3/4/92 To Arkansas Eastman 5/1/93
	4927	3/57	22833	Orig. CVR To GTW GPR9 4618 4/17/91
	4928	12/57	23995	Phase III Orig. CVR to GTW GPR9 4620 6/30/91
	4929(2)	6/55	20316	Ex-BN 1855, né NP 229 To GTW 3/29/88 To Rail Switching Service 2/11/89

	NUMBER	DATE FINISHED	FRAME #	NOTES
Battle Creek Rebuilt GPR9	4605	8/9/89	5512-5	Ex-CV 4551
	4606	10/31/89	5514-8	Ex-GTW 4914
	4607	12/14/89	5512-4	Ex-CV 4550
	4608	12/21/89	5512-10	Né-CV 4556
	4609	3/30/90	5510-3	Ex-CV 4925
	4610	4/30/90	5444-3	Né-GT-NEL 4904
	4611	6/27/90	5512-6	Né-CV 4552
	4612	8/3/90	5510-1	Ex-CV 4923

	MODEL NUMBER	BUILT	BUILDER'S NUMBER	NOTES
GP-38AC	5800	11/71	37929	Ex-GTW
	5801	11/71	37930	Ex-GTW
	5802	11/71	37931	Ex-GTW
	5803	11/71	37932	Ex-GTW Wrecked Sharon, VT 8/7/90 Scrapped
	5804	11/71	37933	Ex-GTW Wrecked Sharon, VT 8/7/90 Repaired at Battle Creek
	5805	11/71	37934	Ex-GTW
	5806	11/71	37935	Ex-GTW
	5807	11/71	37936	Ex-GTW Wrecked Sharon, VT 8/7/90 Repaired at Altoona, PA, by Conrail
	5808	11/71	37937	Same as 5807
	5809	11/71	37938	Same as 5807
	5810	11/71	37939	Ex-GTW
	5811	11/71	37940	Ex-GTW
	6209	4/70	36338	Ex-DT&I 209
	6217	7/71	36868	Ex-DT&I 217
SD-38	6250	1969	34863	Ex-DT&I Used on Sprint train
	6253	7/71	36872	Ex-DT&I Used on Sprint train

REFERENCES:
1. Extra 2200 South, CN System Roster in Issues 48, 49, 50.
2. Canadian Trackside Guide, 1994.
3. Personal contact with many CV employees, including (but not limited to): George Harmon, Tim Caswell, Bob Yarger, Louis Preston, and especially Skip Lehmann, Jim Concannon, and Jim Murphy.
4. Ken Lanovich of Chicago was an invaluable source of information from the GTW. He graciously proofread the roster for me, pointing out several pieces of new information and (I am embarrassed to admit) correcting a few errors!
5. I would like to especially thank Bob Harmon, retired CV Mechanical Officer, who reviewed the roster and chronology for accuracy.

Any remaining errors are mine! Please correct any errors that you detect by writing:
Alan Irwin 5 Wildwood Drive Essex Jct., VT 05452-3815

TONNAGE RATINGS

BETWEEN	Cantic and North Jct.	St. Albans and Essex Jct.	Essex Jct. and Montpelier Jct.	Montpelier Jct. and Roxbury	Roxbury and White River Jct.	White River Jct. and Brattleboro	Brattleboro and Amherst	Amherst and Palmer	Palmer and Willimantic	Willimantic and New London	St. Albans and Richford	Essex Jct. and Burlington
SERIES	\multicolumn{12}{c}{SOUTHWARD}
*3602–GR-17 *3614–GR-17 *4100-4952–GR-17	1810	2170	2140	1600	2400	2100	1600	1050	1250	1600	950	2620
5800-5849–GR-20	2440	2610	2495	2175	2740	2330	1835	1600	1600	1865	985	2800
**5500-5610–GR-20 **9302-9315–GR-430 **9400-9667–GF-430	2900	3290	3160	2800	3450	2980	2410	2090	3100	2440	1445	3500
SERIES	\multicolumn{12}{c}{NORTHWARD}
*3602––GR-17 *3614––GR-17 *4100-4952–GR-17	2100	2240	2865	2865	2145	2040	1430	1430	2210	1390	955	1575
5800-5849–GR-20	2550	2640	3330	3330	2495	2330	1635	1635	2520	1590	1085	1800
**5500-5610–GR-20 **9302-9315–GR-430 **9400-9667–GF-430	2795	3030	3815	3815	2860	2670	1885	1885	2890	1830	1245	2070
CAR FACTOR:	7	7	6	6	6	7	4	4	4	5	3	4

CENTRAL VERMONT RAILWAY DIESEL CHRONOLOGY 1980–1995

Prepared by Alan Irwin, June 1995

1/1/80	Locomotives assigned to St. Albans:	
	RS-11	3600, 3601, 3602, 3603, 3604, 3605, 3609(2), 3611, 3612, 3614
	GP-9	4442, 4445, 4447, 4450, 4548, 4549, 4550, 4551, 4558, 4559
	GP-9	4923, 4924, 4925, 4926, 4927, 4928
	SW-1200	1509, 1510, 1511
	S-4	8081

1/3–13/80　　VTR GP-38-2 "George D. Aiken" used on the *Rocket* as a trial. GT 4558 used by VTR.

7/29/80　　4924 released after rebuilding at St. Albans. Had suffered engine fire on 1/5/80. Rebuilt with dual controls for service on the *Rocket*.
　　Other rebuilds: 4442 3/20/81
　　　　　　　　　4445 Early July 1981
　　　　　　　　　4926 with chopped nose, 9/24/84. Dimensions of the chopped nose of 3608 used as a pattern. 3608 had been rebuilt by DWP in Virginia, MN.
　　　　　　　　　4559 with chopped and yellow nose, 12/2/86

7/80　　3609(1) cannibalized. Cut up 4/81.

1/20–25/81　　VTR GP-38-2 201 "Jay Wulfson" leased to CV for a power shortage. No CV unit on VTR.

3/12/81　　Pusher service started on Freight 444. 1-2 locomotives would go as far as Roxbury.

6/81　　DWP 3612 had engine replaced by CN at Moncton, N.B.

11/4/81　　Locomotive swap with VTR. CV 4551, 4558 delivered to Burlington and VTR 201, 202 picked up. CV wanted to see if 2 GP-38-2's could replace 3 GP-9's. (They could not.)
　　　　　11/12/81 VTR 201 returned in exchange for CV 4558 (201 Built 12/72 B/N 72665-1)
　　　　　11/15/81 VTR 202 returned. CV 4551 picked up 11/16/81 (202 Built 10/74 B/N 75603-1)

11/24/81　　Wreck at Northfield Farms, MA. CV 4447, 4450, 4928 wrecked when a vandal left a switch open. 4447, 4450 repaired relatively quickly. 4928 had severe cab and short hood damage. Short hood and cab from CR GP-9 #5938, ex-EL 1208 used to repair 4928. Returned to service 10/10/83.

11/2/82　　CV-B&M locomotive pool ended.

11/1/82 to 1/6/83　　CN power used exclusively on 444-447. (Too expensive at one cent per horsepower per hour plus fuel.) Used intermittently until 4/3/83. GP-9's cost $500 per month.

1/83　　CV considered leasing a B&LE SD-7 to switch Italy Yard. Used MU'd SW-1200's instead.

3-5/83　　Major locomotive swap within Grand Trunk Corporation. CV was for sale.
　　DWP to CV: 3606, 3607 (u/s), 3608, 3610 (u/s), 3613 arrived St. Albans 4/12/83.
　　　　All in DWP Blue paint. 3607, 3610 never placed in service—both scrapped in Italy Yard 6/85.
　　CV to GTW: 4450, 4549, 4923 left St. Albans 5/1/83 and placed in storage on GTW. Never used by GTW. 4450 returned to CV 3/24/84. 4549 rebuilt at Battle Creek and returned to CV 7/2/84. CV no longer for sale.
　　GTW to DWP: 5850, 5851, 5852, 5853. All ex-RI GP-38-2's.

9/28–29/83　　VTR 201 rented for one round trip on the *Rocket*. Wreck had trapped too much CV power on Southern Division.

2/7/84　　BN 1855 arrived St. Albans. Became CV 4929 (2) before entering service on 2/1/84. Bought from Chrome Locomotive.

7/27/84　　RI 1345 arrived from Chrome Locomotive. Entered service 8/9/84 as CV 3602 (2).

7/28/84　　RI 1334 arrived from Chrome Locomotive. Entered service 8/2/84 as CV 3614 (2). RS-11's 3602 (1) and 3614 (1) retired and stored.

4/15/85	GT 4441, 4448 arrive St. Albans
9/26/85	P&W GP-38 2010 used as test for the upcoming *Quasar* to see if one GP-38 could handle the tonnage. It could not.
11/85	CV 3606, 3611 leased to Quaboag Transfer for service on the *Quasar*. First run of the *Quasar* 11/17/85. Both units in QT green and gold.
4/21/86 to 5/16/86	Guilford strike affected CV traffic, requiring more power. VTR 801GP-18, ex-TP&W 600 leased until 5/3/86. CV had wanted two GP-38-2's.
4/25/86	GT 5808, 4917 arrived St. Albans. First GTW GP-38-AC assigned to St. Albans. 4917 returned 8/88

4/86	VTR operated wayfreights on the CV during the GTI strike, when CV workers would not cross picket lines. Engines used by VTR crews on the CV:
	    GP-38-2 VTR #202
	    SW-1500 VTR 501, CLP 502 (ex-TP&W 304)
	    GP-9 VTR 751 (ex-CR 7301), CLP 752 (ex-BN 1879)

7/5/86 to 10/31/86	GT 6253 (SD-38) arrived in St. Albans for use on Sprint cable-laying train. Used because of its slow speed controls. Is an ex-DT&I hump engine from Flat Rock, MI.
9/6/86	QT 1701 (ex P&W 1701, ex PRR, PC, CR 7189 GP-9 b/n 24222, 11/57) and P&W 1702 (ex PRR, PC, CR, GP-9 7205) tested on *Quasar*. QT was considering buying 1702 if the two units could pull the *Quasar*. Crew had to double Slip Hill in Waterbury and Roxbury!
9/11/86	CV 4550 was the first unit with the yellow-nose version of the Larson-Mumley green paint scheme, 10/4/86. CV 4926 painted in low-nose version of the yellow nose for director's special. 4559 rebuild not yet completed as originally planned.
10/6/86	QT 3611 suffered an engine explosion. (The explosion occurred while QT President Kirk Bryant was talking to the Champlain Valley Chapter NRHS!)
10/21/86	QT 3606 hit propane truck (little damage).

11/7/86	Two ex-CR GP-38's arrive for *Quasar*. Never repainted.
	    7803 10/69 B/N 35432
	    7822 11/69 B/N 35451

12/4-5/86	CN 9408 made round trip to New London. First GP-40-2W south of St. Albans.

11/5/87	GTW 4100's start arriving on CV. Phase III GP-9 freight units without dynamic brakes. CV wanted 12 GP-38's
	    11/5/87 4135, 4136, 4138
	    11/11/87 4137
	    11/16/87 4139
	    7/15/88 4134

12/4/87	K&L Feeds #1 (ex-CV 8081) left for Yantic, CT.
1/13/88	Last southbound *Quasar*. Last northbound *Quasar* 1/14/88. CR 7803, 7822 used by CV in general freight service. To Genessee and Wyoming 3/14/88. Used on the Buffalo and Pittsburgh.
2/88	GT 5800-class GP-38AC's start arriving in quantity.
3/8/88	CV 3608, 3612, and 3601 (u/s for parts) sold to LVRC. 3601 was the only RS-11 to get yellow nose paint.
3/29/88	CV 4929 (2) left for GTW.
6/1/88	All RS-11's off Grand Trunk New England Lines. Replaced by GT 4136, 4441, 4448, CV 4442.
6/16/88	CV 3600 and 3604 to Genessee Valley Leasing Co. 3603 for parts followed 10/89.

8/15/88	CV 4542 arrived in St. Albans. Rumor had it that the unit was painted "CV" by mistake. Another unit had been planned for the CV, but 4542 was sent.
8/22/88	CV 4559 dedicated to George J. Harmon, the recently deceased CV Mechanical Officer. Mr. Harmon was responsible for the GP-9 rebuilding program in St. Albans.
9/10/88	CV took over operation of the Conn River Line from B&M.
10/7/88	CV 3605, QT 3606, CV 3609 (2), QT 3611 (u/s) left St. Albans for Winchester and Western, Gore, VA. 3605 still there. 3606 wrecked May 1994 as Wimpey Minerals 360, Annville, PA. 3609 now Maine Coast 367. 3611 scrapped on W&W.
11/30/88	CV 1509, 1510, 1511 to GTW.
1/4/89	CV 4551 sent to Battle Creek for repairs. Rebuilt into GP-9R 4605. Eventually all CV GP-9's sent to GTW.
2/16/89	CV-Blue 4557 arrived in St. Albans. Bought new by CV 3/57. Had been on GTW since 1/65.
5/22/89	First day of operation of St. Lawrence and Atlantic (former Grand Trunk-New England) Power: GT-Blue 4441, 4448, CV-Green 4442, 4445, 4447, 4450. 4442-4450 originally dieselized the GT-NEL in 6/56!
6/1/89	GT 4922 arrived. Returned 8/16/89. On CV again 10/15/89-11/6/89. Eventually 4912 and 4917-4922 all on CV. All painted GT Blue. None ever CV.
7/17/89	Press run of the *Montrealer*. First revenue run 7/18/89.
10/27/89	CV 4548 to GTW. Leased to Huron and Eastern as 105. Now Delaware Valley 105.
11/5/89	GT 4600 rebuilds start arriving. None ever got a "CV." First was 4605, ex-CV 4551.
1990	Many locomotive moves as GP-9's were sent to GTW for 4600 rebuild program and 5800's and 4600's replaced them.
8/7/90	Washout at Sharon, VT. 5803 Wrecked and retired. 5807, 5808, 5809 rebuilt by CR shops at Altoona, PA. 5804 repaired at Battle Creek. GT 5810, 5811, 6209, 6217 hastily sent to the CV. All GP-38AC's.
9/6/90	CV 4549 sent to GTW. Was the last of the original, unmodified CV GP-9's left on CV. As of 5/95, only 4548 as Delaware Valley 105 is left unaltered!
9/3/91	CV 3602 (2) and 3614 (2) to GTW.
1990–1992	All CV power was 5800's, 4600's, CV 4926, CV 4559, CV 3602 (2), CV 3614 (2).
3/1/92	Last use of CV power on 444–447. CN run-through power started 3/3/92. Within 2 months all non GP-38AC's gone to GTW. Mostly CN GP-40, GP-40-2W, GTW GP-38 and GP-38-AC's, EMD Leasing ex-CR GP-38's, GATX 3702 (GP-40), EMD Leasing 200-201 (GP-40).
3/4/92	CV 4559 and 4926 to GTW. General Manager Chris Burger had wanted to keep them as "publicity" units because of their green and yellow CV paint.
3/9/92 to 4/9/92	All GT 4600's left for GTW.
10/9–24/92	GT 6250 (SD-38) laid Sprint cable 10 miles north from New London. The night it arrived, the southbound *Montrealer* broke down. 6250 pulled an empty passenger train as a deadhead move to the Southern Division. (It's rare to see an SD-38 on "varnish.")
1/16/94	First use of 6-wheel truck power on CV. Mostly CN SD-40, SD-40-2W, ex-UP SD-40-2, ex-CSX (né Clinchfield) HATX SD-45-2. Once CN 2402. Rarely CN HR-616. After 9/94, LMS C40-8W. Rebuilt CN SD-40's in 6000 series common.
2/3/95	Last full day of operation of Central Vermont Railway after 122 years. Power on hand: CV 5800, CV 5801, GT 5802, GT 5806 CV 5807, CV 5808, CV 5809, CV 5810.

Index

Note: Page numbers in *italic* refer to photograph captions.

Act 250, 154
Admiralty Group Limited, 39
Agway, *50, 166*
Alden Corporation, 84
Amestoy, Jeffrey, 155
Amherst, MA, 33, 75, *77, 78*
Amtrak (*see also* Montrealer), 8, *12,* 16, 21–23, 26, 34, 35, 39, *39, 44, 47,* 48, 51, 75, 90, 92, 94, 99, 102, *103,* 107, 117, *119, 124, 138,* 162, 165
    superliner coaches, *159*
    termination of the *Montrealer,* 162, 165
Anderson, Fred, 157

Bagby, Ken, 51
Barkyoumb, Ken, *48*
Barretts, MA, 23, 26, *83*
Bean, Bobby, *33*
Belchertown, MA, 5, 11, 23, 36, *61, 134, 149*
    vote on automobile distribution facility, 46
Bellows Falls, VT, *12, 68,* 75, 80, 99, *107, 109, 114, 119, 121, 132, 138, 160*
Bliss, Jack, *81*
Boardman, D. W., 67
Bombardier, Inc., 34, 38, *60*
Boston & Maine Railroad (B&M) (*see also* Guilford Transportation Industries), 3, *3, 6,* 8, *8,* 10, *12,*

Boston & Maine Railroad (B&M) (*continued*)
    13, 16,*17, 25,* 26, *26, 26,* 27, *28, 29,* 35, 38, 39, *41, 43,* 48, *49, 57, 66,* 92, *126*
Boston, MA, 2, 8, 11
Boucher, Ron, 54
Bourdeau, Mike, *16*
Braintree, VT, 5
Brattleboro, VT, 3, *6,* 10, 13, *20, 26,* 35, 39, 40, *49,* 51, *57, 86,* 102, *112, 122, 128–129, 137, 140,* 165, 167, 169
Bridges
    East Alburg trestle, 2, *4,* 5, 13, *54, 103, 153, 158, 160*
    Sugar River Bridge (Claremont High Bridge), *4, 64, 118, 133*
    Duxbury Bridge, *32, 89, 122, 132, 167*
    East Northfield Bridge, *75*
    Georgia High Bridge, *13, 79, 89, 158*
    Millers Falls Bridge, *136*
    Sheldon Junction Bridge, 15–16, *43,* 46
    Windsor (VT)-Cornish (NH) Bridge, *143*
    Winooski River Bridge, Essex Junction, *153*
Brigham, Mike, *169*
Bruso, Al, 40
Bryant, Kirk, *81*
Buildings
    Amtrak Station, Essex Junction, *34*
    B&M Station, Westminster, *28*

Buildings *(continued)*
    Boston & Albany freight house, Palmer, MA, *80*
    Car repair facility, St. Albans, *39*
    Enginehouse, St. Albans, *16, 40, 41, 67, 76, 163*
    Office Building, Palmer, MA, 42
    Office Building, St. Albans, *69, 81, 168*
    Roundhouse, White River Junction, 33
    Scale House, St. Albans, *50*
    Station, Amherst, MA, *78*
    Station, Bellows Falls, *12, 68*
    Station, Brattleboro, *26*
    Station, Chester (GMRC), *119*
    Station, East Georgia, *13*
    Station, Montpelier Junction, *22, 103*
    Station, Palmer, MA, *29*
    Station, South Coventry, CT, *23*
    Station, Stafford Springs, CT, *121*
    Station, Swanton, *71*
    Yard Office, Palmer, MA, *30*
Burger, Christopher J., 76, 92, 102, 105, *110*, 118, 139, *146*, 155–156, 160
Burlington Electric Department (*see also* McNeil Generating Plant), 13, 25
Burlington Free Press, 150
Burlington, VT, 8, *11*, 23, 25, 30, 39, *53, 96*, 102, *149, 155*, 165
    waterfront property dispute and sale, 82, 84, 87–88, 94, 99, 102, 107

Camp Drum, NY, 21
Canadian National Railway (CN), 1, *2*, 10, 11, 14, 42, 46, *47*, 72, 75, 80, 82, *97, 98*, 107
    Canadian National North America (CNNA), 107, 114, 118, 140, 143, 154–155, 156
    strike on, 40, 42
Canadian Pacific Railway (CPR), *6*, 8, 15, 16, *20, 43*, 46, 92
Canfor USA Corporation, 72
Canon, D. J., 167
Celetano, P. A., 167
Central of Indiana Railroad, 156
Central of Indianapolis Railroad, 156
Central Properties (Kokomo, IN), 156
Central Vermont Railway
    commodities handled
        "A" turbine rotor (Vermont Yankee), *161*
        cement, 3, 5, 11, 36, 46, 72
        chemicals and fuels, 27, 38, 72, *134*
        flyash, 80, 99, *152*
        limestone, *108, 132*
        lumber (*see also* Quasar), 2, 3, 11, 13, 27, 36, 46, *71*, 72, *89, 93, 97*, 110
        M-1 tanks, 160
        milk, 2
        paper/newsprint, 13, 26, 36, 46, 72, 110, 140
        plastics, 38, 72

Central Vermont Railway
    commodities handled *(continued)*
        steel, 38, 99
        subway cars (*see* Bombardier, Inc.)
        U.S. Mail, 5, *9*
        wheat, 99
        wire/copper, 3, 27, 110
        wood pulp, 72, 76
    computers and, 33–34
    derailments and other accidents, 15–16, 19, 21–23, 27, 30, 40, 42, *43, 44, 45*, 46, 48, *61*, 72, 75, *91*, 92, *93, 101, 104, 109*
    farewell party, *165*
    financial performance, 1, 5–6, 11, 14–15, 33, 38, 43, 46, 72, 80, 82, 99, 107, 117, 118, 140
    labor relations, 14, 25–26, 34–35, 46, 54, 92, 105
    last day of operations, *134, 164*, 165, *166*, 167, *167, 168*, 169
    Northern Division, 1, 8, 13, 42, 72, 160, 165
    proposed sale of, 10, 118
    Safety Incentive Plan, 157
    sale to RailTex, 143
    Southern Division, 1, 2, 3, 8, 10, 13, 23, 27, 42, 43, 54, 72, *111, 136*, 165
    track maintenance and improvement, 2, 5, 10, 13–14, 33, 42, *55*, 72, 80, 90, 92, 102, 105, 107, 115, 117, *158*
    Transportation Center (Italy Yard), 88, 90
    yard inventory system, 13
Central Vermont Railway Historical Society, 157
Central Vermont RHS Convention, *110*
Charlestown, NH, *7*, 25, *41, 62–63, 94, 116, 126, 156*
Cheney, Ernie, 158
Chesapeake & Ohio Railroad (C & O), *6*
Chicago & North Western Railroad, 139, 160
Chicago, IL, 3, 140, 165
Chrome Crankshaft (Silvis, IL), 165
Church, Vernon, 19, 21
Claremont Junction, NH, *28, 113*
Claremont, NH, *4, 64, 133*
Clavelle, Peter, 102
Coffin, Vic, 34
Colchester, VT, 21, *51, 53*, 80, *145, 148*
Coleman, Frank, *110*
Coleman, Tim, *110*
Concord, NH, 102
Conn River Line (B&M), *25, 26*
    appeal to forced sale and U.S. Supreme Court decision, 92, 94
    deterioration of, 38–39
    disputed sale to CV and rehabilitation, 48, 51–52, 54, 102
    Golden Spike Ceremony, 52, 54
Connecticut Yankee (Amtrak bus service), 75
Conrail, 14, 27, *29*, 35, 38, 40, 72, *80*, 110, *120*
Constantine, Howard, *48*

Cornish, NH, 102, *143*
CSF Acquisition Group (Morrisville, VT), 143
CSX Corporation, 80

Daley, D. J., 169
Davis, Jim, 150, *169*
Dean, Howard, 162, 165
Delaware & Hudson Railroad (D&H) (*see also* Guilford Transportation Industries), 3, 10, 11, 14, 35, 80
DesLauriers, Peter, 150
Detroit, MI, 105, 157
Downs, Thomas, 162, 165
Duchesneau, Michael, 118, 157
Duffany, Ray, 51
Duluth, Winnipeg & Pacific Railway Company (DW&P), 1, 13, 105
Dummerston, VT, *104*
Duxbury, VT, *32, 89, 122, 132, 167*

Eagleville, CT, *127*
East Alburg, VT, 5, 13, *31, 32,* 36
East Berkshire, VT, *100,* 117
East Cambridge, MA, 13
East Georgia, VT, *13*
East Highgate, VT, *141*
East Northfield, MA, *12, 75, 123*
East Northfield, VT, 10
Emergency Response Training Program (Amtrak), 16
Employee Stock Ownership Plan (ESOP), 118, 139, 143
Enosburg, VT, 10, 117
Environmental Protection Agency (EPA), 80
Essex Junction, VT, *3, 8,* 19, 30, *34, 38,* 40, *73,* 80, *86,* 102, 107, *137, 147, 153,* 160
"Ethan Frome" (film), *115*

Faucett, Tom, 51, 156
Federal Railroad Administration, 51
Flanagan, Mike, *110, 131,* 167
Flock Fibers, Inc. (FFI), *154*
Flohr, Bruce, 146, 147, 150
Florida West Coast Railroad, 143
Fonda Junction, VT, 46, *93*

Garceau, Roger, *16*
Garvey, Ed, 146, 150, 155
Gay, George E., 6, 19, *58*
Georgia, VT, 13, *27*
Gibson, Ty, 51
Gifford Memorial Hospital (Randolph, VT), 92
"Glory Days of Railroading" celebration, *126, 159*
Golden Freight Car Award, 25
Goulette, Paul, 19
Graham, Rosalyn, 80
Grand Trunk Corporation (GTC), 1, 10, 11, 13, 51,

Grand Trunk Corporation (GTC) *(continued)* 76, *97,* 107, 139, 143, 147, 157
Grand Trunk Western Railroad Company (GTW), 1, 11, 46
Graves, Carlton, 40
Green Mountain Air Freight, 33
Green Mountain Flyer, 68
Green Mountain Railroad (GMRC), *68,* 80, 99, *107, 109, 119*
Guilford Transportation Industries (GTI) (*see also* Boston & Maine Railroad, Delaware & Hudson Railroad, and Maine Central Railroad), 10, 11, 14, 34, 35, 39, 48, 51
strike on, 34–36

H. K. Webster feed mill, 15
Harmon, Bob, *81,* 99, *99*
Harmon, George J., *99*
Harrison, NJ, 38
Hartford, CT, 8
Hartland, VT, 8, *82*
Heald, Randy, 19
Hebda, Jerry, *146*
Howard, Jeff, 19
Hulcher Professional Services, Inc. (Gettysburg, PA), 21, 23, 46, 92, *93*
Hurricane Gloria, 30, 33

Independent Cement Company, 11, 23
Interstate Commerce Commission (ICC), 10, 15, 48, 51, 92, 94, 117, 139, 140, 147, 150, 151, 154, 155, 165
Italy Yard (St. Albans), 2, *2, 7,* 8, *14, 15, 17, 33, 39,* 46, *50, 74, 77,* 89–90, *91, 98,* 105, *109, 130, 134, 148*

Jacobs, Lyle, *48*
Jeffords, James, 39, 40, *86,* 140, 147, 150, 155, 162
Jones, Bob, *40*
Jordan spreader, *130, 148*

Kenyon, Don, *48*
Kunin, Madeleine, 39, 40, 75

Labor Strategies, Inc. (Madison, WI), 146
Ladd, Paul, 40
Lamoille Valley Railroad Corporation (LVRC), 23, 46, 48, *97, 100,* 117, *141,* 143
LaPerle, Maurice, 157
Larner, Paul, 157
Larson, Phillip C., 15, 39, 46, 51, 52, 76, *86*
Leahy, Patrick, 48, 52, 54, 75, 140, 147, 150, 155, 162
Lemay, H. G., 19
Leverett, MA, 30
Lewis Rail Service, 5
Livingston, Roger P., 3, 167

THE CENTRAL VERMONT RAILWAY   179

Locomotives
 Diesel
  Amtrak 211, *44*
  Amtrak 401, 54
  CL&P 752, *65*
  CN 2118, *161*
  CN 2548, *47*
  CN 2570, *2*
  CN 2575, *62–63*
  CN 2579, *62–63*
  CN 5034, *149*
  CN 6005, *151*
  CN 9505, 167
  CN 9581, 167
  CN 9625, 167
  CN 9636, *145*
  CN 9649, *118*
  CN 9665, *138*
  CN 9677, *144*
  Conrail Leasing 790, *140*
  CR 7822, *94*
  CV 1509, 20, *30*, 74
  CV 1510, *20*
  CV 1511, 1, *74*
  CV 3602, 72, 77, 80, *110*
  CV 3603, *73*
  CV 3606, 13, 27, *53*, 60, 66, *90*
  CV 3607, 13, *72*
  CV 3608, 13, *34*, 60, *62–63*, 67, 72, 81, *90*
  CV 3609, *28*, 72
  CV 3610, 13, *72*
  CV 3611, 27, *60*, *61*, 66, 72, *83*
  CV 3612, *53*, *62–63*
  CV 3613, 13, *72*
  CV 3614, 72, *76*, 77, 80, *94*
  CV 4134, *106*
  CV 4442, 1
  CV 4445, *94*
  CV 4447, *18*, *62–63*, 94
  CV 4448, *80*
  CV 4450, 11, *75*
  CV 4450, *80*
  CV 4548, *62–63*
  CV 4549, 11, *18*, *57*, *62–63*
  CV 4550, *62–63*
  CV 4551, *57*, *64*, *78*
  CV 4558, 2, *18*, 68
  CV 4559 ("George J. Harmon"), 52, *67*, *68*, *70*, *98*, *101*, *111*, *120*
   dedication ceremony, *99*
  CV 4917, *88*
  CV 4923, 11, *21*, *80*
  CV 4924, 1, *8*, *21*, *80*, *94*
  CV 4925, *18*, *29*, *62–63*, *78*
  CV 4926, *41*, *52*, *59*, *67*, *76*, *78*, *86*, *102*, *112*
  CV 4928, *37*, *62–63*, *98*, *106*

Locomotives (*continued*)
  CV 4929, *50*, *62–63*, *65*
  CV 5800, *113*, *135*, 169
  CV 5801, *115*, *164*, 167
  CV 5802, *111*, *135*, 169
  CV 5803, *109*
  CV 5804, *104*, *109*
  CV 5806, *111*, *136*, 169
  CV 5807, *109*
  CV 5809, *109*, *135*, 169
  CV 5810, *126*, *130*, *149*, *163*, *166*, 167
  CV 6209, *111*
  CV 8081, *35*, *37*, *65*
  GMRC 1849, *132*
  GMRC 1851, *138*
  GMRC 401, *65*
  GT 3604, 55
  GT 4136, *106*
  GT 4606, *107*
  GT 4918, *112*
  GT 5808, 36, 54, *70*, *94*, *98*, *105*, *109*, *136*, *161*
  GT 6253, 36, *84*
  K&L Feeds 1, *92*
  LV 3612, *100*
  NEC 9521, 167
  NEC 9530, 167
  NEC 9531, 167
  NEC 9536, 167
  NEC 9549, 167
  Speno 121 (RMS-12 rail-grinder), *108*
  VTR 201, 2
  VTR 202, 2, *12*
  VTR 801, *60*, *61*, *62–63*
 Steam
  B&M 4-4-0 494, *126*
  CV 4-6-0 220, 160
  UP "Big Boy" 4012, *49*
  Valley Railroad 2-8-2 142, *115*
Locomotive & Railway Preservation magazine, 98
Long Island Sound, 5, 56
Luman, Robert, 6

Maas, Gerald, 52, 76
Maine Central Railroad (*see also* Guilford Transportation Industries), 10, 34, 35, *57*
Maple Leaf (newsprint distribution center), 26
Massachusetts Central Railroad, 140, 165
Mass Bay Railroad Enthusiasts, *35*, *138*
Maynard, Bobby, 42
McMahon, N. J., 169
McNeil Generating Plant (*see also* Burlington Electric Department), 23, 46, *53*, *73*, 155
Metro North Commuter Railroad, 34
Middlesex, VT, 30, 52, 54, *116*
Miller Construction Company, 115
Millers Falls, MA, *17*, *66*, *136*

Milton, VT, *18, 58,* 80, *108, 133, 145*
Missisquoi Bay, VT, 5
Missisquoi Pulp Mill (Boise Cascade), 15
Modern Railroads magazine, 25, 27
Monson, MA, 26, *31,* 36, *67, 87, 88*
Montpelier Junction, VT, 8, *22,* 34, 36, 38, 40, *103, 161, 166*
Montpelier, VT, 26
Montreal, Quebec, 5, *7,* 13, 14, 35, 46, 75, 76, 114, 115, 165, 167
Montville, CT, 80, 99, *152*
Morrisville, VT, 48
Mud Pond (VT), *48, 64, 84, 117*
Murphy, Jim, 54, *110*

National Transportation Safety Board (NTSB), 22
New England Central Railroad Company, Inc. (*see also* RailTex), 150, 151, 154, 157, 162, 165, 167, 169, *169*
  first day of operations, 169
New England Warehouse (newsprint distribution center), 26
New Hampshire & Vermont Railroad, 143
New Haven, CT, 11
New Jersey Transit Corporation, 34, 38
New London, CT, 3, *5,* 10, 13, 23, 33, 35, 39, 54, *56,* 75, 80, 115, *135, 152,* 169
Newport, VT, 16
Norfolk Southern Railroad, 40
North Belchertown, MA, *111*
North Monson, MA, *35, 49*
North Walpole, NH, *74, 105, 124, 154*
North Williston, VT, *87, 95*
Northern Barns, 33
Northfield, VT, 6, *24, 42*
Norwich, CT, 3, 23, 33, 36, *131*
Noyen, Quebec, 36

Oakes Development (St. Louis Park, MN), 143
Oakland, VT, 40, *69, 91, 106, 159*
Olmstead, Mike, 157
Operation Lifesaver, 26, *107, 155*
  "Trooper on the Train," 80
Oppenheimer, Wolff, and Donnelly (Chicago, IL), 118
Ovitt, Jack, 51, 157

Palmer, MA, 1, 3, 8, 13, *18,* 23, 27, *29, 30,* 33, 35, 36, 38, 40, 42, 43, 48, 54, *65, 78,* 80, *83,* 92, *96, 101, 104, 106,* 110, *112,* 114, 115, *115, 118, 120, 123, 136,* 140, *144, 164,* 167, 169
Pangborn, Lee, 46
Paquette,—, *48*
Phelps-Dodge Corporation, 3
PMI Lumber Transfer, 72
Poulin, N. J., 169

Preston, Louis, *16*
Providence & Worcester Railroad, 5, 140
Putney, VT, *108*

Quaboag Lumber, 23
Quaboag Transfer, Inc., 27
Quilliam, Wayne J., *141,* 167

R. S. Audley Company, 107
RailTex (San Antonio, TX) (*see also* New England Central Railroad), 143, 146, 150, 154
  opposition to RailTex purchase of CV, 146–147, 150–151, 154, 155, 165
Railway Labor Act, 35
Randolph, VT, 3, 40
Reagan, Ronald, 35
Richford Branch, 8, 10, 15, 16, *43,* 46, *100, 110*
  abandonment of, 117, *141*
Richford, VT, *20,* 46, 48, 117
Richmond Cooperative Creamery, 2
Richmond, VT, *44, 98, 162*
Rivers, J. J., 167
Rivers, M. A., 167
Roberge, W. A., 167
Roberts, Bud, *48*
Rouses Point, NY, 8
Roxbury Hill (VT), 3
Roxbury, VT, (*see also* Mud Pond) *24, 90, 124, 131, 144, 146, 157*
Royalton, VT, 72
Runyon, L. D., 169
Rutland Railroad, *11*
  Rutland Railroad Combine 260, *119, 159*
Rutland, VT, 35, 165

Saint Albans Historical Society, 157
Saint Albans, VT, 1, 2, 3, 5, 8, *9,* 11, 13, *16, 19, 21,* 23, 26, 27, 30, 34, 35, *37,* 38, 42, 43, 46, *47,* 48, 52, *55, 60, 67,* 69, *70, 71,* 75, 80, *81, 85,* 92, *92, 97,* 102, *110, 113, 114,* 115, 140, 146, 147, 150, 151, *163, 164,* 165, *165, 166,* 167, *168,* 169
Sanders, Bernard, 140, 147, 150, 155, 162
Santa Train, 42–43, *111*
Sarnia, Ontario, 46
Saxonville Lumber Company, *25*
Sharon, VT, *35,* 36, 72, 92, 115, 117
Shelburne Museum (Shelburne, VT), 160
Sheldon Junction, VT, 10, 16, *43,* 46, 117, *141*
Sheldon Springs, VT, 15
Slip Hill (VT), *59*
Smith Cove, CT, *125*
Smith, Hubert, 6
Snelling, Richard, 21
South Charlestown, NH, *95, 102, 142, 151*
South Coventry, CT, *23*
South Willington, CT, *55*

South Windham, CT, 3, 36
Special Collections (University of Vermont), 157
Springfield Terminal Railway, *25, 41*
Springfield, MA, 5, 8, 10, 26, 34, 35, 38, 39, 75
Stafford Springs, CT, *58, 115, 121*
Stafford, CT, 10, 90
Staggers Act, 1
State Line, MA, *65, 88*
Swanton, VT, 8, 13, 23, 25, 46, *71*
Szabo, L. J., 167, 169

Thibault, S. A., 165
Thompson, Charles, 102
Three Rivers, MA, *61*
Toronto, Ontario, 140
Trains
   Burlington wayfreight, *11, 96, 137, 145, 155*
   Hay Train, 39–40, *86*
   Montrealer (*see also* Amtrak), 8, *13*, 34, 38, 39, *44*, 75, 76, *87, 88*, 102, *116, 124, 147*, 162, *162, 164*, 165, 169
     derailment in Williston, VT, 19, 21–23, *44, 45*
     numbering change, 117
   NEC Train 323, 169
   NEC Train 554, 169
   Quasar (Quaboag lumber train), 42, 46, 48, *60, 64, 66*, 90
   Rocket (intermodal Train 22), 1, 2, *4*, 5, 7, 8, 11, 12, 15, *19*, 25, *28, 37*
   Train 26, 8
   Train 27, 8
   Train 244, *66, 83*
   Train 323, *70*, 117, *123, 125, 126, 131, 133, 142, 144, 153, 159, 160, 161*, 165, *166*, 167, *168*
   Train 324, *114*, 117, *117*, 122, 123, *128–129, 130, 131, 132, 135, 137, 138, 139*, 140, *140, 143, 146, 148, 151, 154, 156, 157*, 160, 165, *166*, 167, *167, 168*
   Train 444, 3, *3*, 8, *8*, 13, *15, 17, 18, 21*, 22, *22*, 24, 29, 31, 32, 34, 39, 42, 45, 46, 47, 48, *48*, 50, 54, 58, 67, 68, 69, 71, *81*, 87, 89, 90, 93, 94, 96, *103, 104, 106, 113*, 114, *114*, 116, 117, 119, 122, 124, *133, 146, 153*
   Train 447, 2, *4*, 7, 8, 27, 32, 38, 39, 41, *59*, 62–63, 64, 68, 69, 72, 74, 75, *82, 85*, 89, *91*, 92, 94, 95, 98, *101, 102, 105, 111, 112*, 114, 117, *121, 151*
   Train 550, *73*
   Train 553, 8
   Train 554, 8, *8, 49*, 165, 169
   Train 555, 8, *120, 121, 125, 127, 131, 135, 136,*

Train 555 (*continued*)
   149, 152, 165, 169
Train 556, *59, 96, 134, 163,* 165, 167
Train 560, 10, *31*
Train 561, 10, *18,* 30, *58*
Train 562, *23, 65, 77, 80, 83, 104, 118, 120, 134, 144,* 165, 167
Woodchip train, 13, 23, 25, 40, 46, *51, 53, 70, 73, 91, 133*
Transportation Communications Union, 54
Trombley, Gene, *141,* 157
Twin State Railroad, 143

U.S. Sprint (fiber optics cable installation), 36, *66, 84*
United Transportation Union (UTU), 54, 140

Valley Railroad, *115*
Valumetrics, Inc., 118
Vermont Army National Guard, 160
Vermont Castings, 3
Vermont Job Service, 46
Vermont Railway (VTR), 2, 8, 11, *12, 17,* 26, 35, *79,* 80, *81,* 82
Vermont Yankee Nuclear Power Plant, *161*
Vernon, VT, 42, *101*

Walker, R. A., 139
Washington County Railroad, 34, 143
Washington, D.C., 35, 75, 151, 154, 162
Washingtonian, 26
Waterbury, J. T., 165
Waterbury, VT, *50, 68, 130*
Websterville, VT, 34, 38
Wells River, VT, 16
West Hartford, VT, *36, 156*
West Swanton, VT, 5
Westminster, VT, *28,* 48, 102, *100, 125, 138*
White River Junction, VT, 1, 3, 8, 10, 13, 19, 26, 27, 33, 35, 38, 39, 40, *44,* 48, *90,* 92, *94,* 102, *126, 139, 159*
Whitehall, NY, 165
Willimantic, CT, 75, 102, *127*
Williston, VT, 19, *44, 45, 151*
Winamac Southern Railroad, 156
Windsor Distribution Terminal, 76
Windsor, VT, 39, 52, 76, 115, *142, 143*
Workers United For Justice, 146
Wyeth Laboratories, 13

Yankee Clipper (Amtrak bus service), 75
Yarger, Bob, *40,* 160

182   THE CENTRAL VERMONT RAILWAY

PALMER SUBDIVISION

Table 1 (Southern portion)

NORTHWARD TRAINS REG. 623 PSGR DAILY	MILEAGE	YARD LIMITS	STATIONS	SIDING CAR CAPACITY	LENGTH OF SIDINGS	SOUTHWARD TRAINS REG. 624 PSGR DAILY
23:15	1.1	1.2	..EAST NEW LONDON...CPZ (Jct. with P.&W.R.R.) 4.9	YARD	YARD	
	6.0		........MONTVILLE....... 6.5	45	2707	
	12.5		......THAMESVILLE...... 0.9	27	1623	
	13.4		........NORWICH........ 3.5			
	16.9		.........YANTIC......... 6.0	21	1293	
	22.9		........LEBANON........ 6.7	YARD	YARD	
	29.6		.......WILLIMANTIC..... (Jct. with P. & W. R.R.) 14.1	34	2040	01:50
	43.7		....WEST WILLINGTON.... 12.0			01:45
01:45	55.7	64.0	.......STATE LINE....... 9.3	85	5106	
01:50	64.8	65.1	.......PALMER....CKPWZ (Jct. with Conrail & MCRR) 4.2	YARD	YARD	
	69.2		.......BARRETTS........ 5.6	32	1938	
	74.8		......BELCHERTOWN...... 10.5			
02:25	85.3		.........AMHERST........P 4.7	60	3620	01:05
	90.0		.........LEVERETT....... 9.6			
	99.6		......MILLERS FALLS..... 11.0			
	110.6		.....EAST NORTHFIELD....P (Jct. with STRR)			

Rules 321-323 applicable.

Table 2 (Northern portion)

NORTHWARD TRAINS REG. 623 PSGR DAILY	MILEAGE	YARD LIMITS	STATIONS	SIDING CAR CAPACITY	LENGTH OF SIDINGS	SOUTHWARD TRAINS REG. 624 PSGR DAILY
	110.6		.....EAST NORTHFIELD.....P (Jct. with STRR) 5.1			
	115.7		.........VERNON......... 5.0	21	1286	
03:15	120.7		.....BRATTLEBORO....BPY 1.3	YARD	YARD	00:15
	122.0		........WEST RIVER...... 7.5	79	4769	
	130.0		.........PUTNEY......... 11.1	162	9732	
	141.1		........WESTMINSTER..... 3.7			
03:50	144.9		......BELLOWS FALLS..... (Jct. with GMRC) 1.1	148	8887	23:40
	146.0		......NORTH WALPOLE..... 6.1			
	152.1		.......CHARLESTOWN...... 9.8			
04:15	161.9		......CLAREMONT JCT...... (Jct. with C&C RR) 8.2	172	10366	23:10
	170.7		.........WINDSOR........ 4.4			
	175.1		........HARTLAND........ 8.3	65	3950	
	183.4		..........BANK.......... (Jct. with STRR) 1.4			
04:50	184.8		.....WHITE RIVER JCT...BPW	YARD	YARD	22:40

Rules 321-323 applicable.